Genetics and
Genetic Engineering

Milestones in Discovery and Invention

Genetics and Genetic Engineering

LISA YOUNT

☑® Facts On File, Inc.

Genetics and Genetic Engineering

Facts On File, Inc.
11 Penn Plaza
New York NY 10001

Library of Congress Cataloging-in-Publication Data
Yount, Lisa.
    Genetics and genetic engineering / Lisa Yount.
p. cm. — (Milestones in discovery and invention)
    Includes bibliographical references and index.
    Summary: Profiles geneticists and highlights discoveries they have made;
    includes Gregor Mendel and the laws of inheritance, James Watson and the
    structure of DNA, and Stanley Cohen and genetic engineering.
    ISBN 0-8160-3566-0
    1. Genetics—History—Juvenile literature. 2. Genetic engineering—History—
Juvenile literature.eni. [1. Genetics. 2. Genetic engineering. 3. Geneticists.]
I. Title. II. Series.
QH437'5.Y68 1997
576.5'09—dc21
                                                97-8891

Facts On File books are available at special discounts when purchased in bulk quantities for businesses, associations, institutions or sales promotions. Please call our Special Sales Department in New York at 212/967-8800 or 800/322-8755.

You can find Facts On File on the World Wide Web at http://www.factsonfile.com

Text design by Cathy Rincon
Cover design by Smart Graphics
Illustrations on pages 8, 21, 26, 30, 46, 49, 50, 62, 88, 91, 92, 109, and 132 by
  Marc Greene

This book is printed on acid-free paper.

Printed in the United States of America

MP FOF 10 9 8 7 6 5 4 3 2

To my parents,
with thanks
for a lively set of genes

. . . .

Contents

. . . .

Introduction

. . . .

They gave the same names to their sons and their dogs. They drive the same kind of car and like the same sports. They both make dollhouse-sized furniture in their basement workshops. In the way they stand, move, and talk, "they [are] so much alike it [is] ridiculous," says the wife of one.

Most people would not be surprised to learn that brothers like these two men have similarities. People expect family members to have quite a bit in common. The surprise comes when people learn that the two men, Jim Lewis and Jim Springer, were separated just a few weeks after their birth. They did not meet again until they were 39 years old.

The two Jims are not merely brothers but identical twins. As brothers, they would have inherited some of the same information from their parents—information that exists as a kind of chemical code in every cell of their bodies, carried in units called genes. As identical twins, they inherited *exactly* the same information.

Scientific study of identical twins raised apart, like the Jim twins, shows how important genes are in determining not only physical characteristics but personality. Such twins often have almost identical scores on a variety of physical and mental tests. Because the twins have been raised by different families, the similarities cannot be due to what they learned from their parents. They have to be due to their genes.

In spite of the striking likeness of people like the Jim twins, scientists know that genes are not everything. What people learn and choose to do during their lifetimes, their experiences, and the people they meet can greatly modify the effect of the genetic information they get from their parents. Someone might inherit genes that give an increased chance of having heart disease, for instance, yet avoid the illness by eating a low-fat diet and exercising often. Research so far suggests that heredity and environment are about equally important in shaping a person's life.

Still, people today are aware as never before of the crucial part that genes play in making them who they are. James Watson, a pioneer in the study of genes, says, "We used to think that our fate was in our stars. Now we know, in large part, that our fate is in our genes." Because genes are so important, discoveries in genetics—the study of genes and the inherited information they contain—potentially affect everyone's life.

Genetics is a creation of the 20th century. Before then, people knew that living things resembled their parents, but they had little idea why. At the start of the century, geneticists (scientists who study genetics) worked out certain rules by which characteristics were inherited. Soon afterward they showed that inherited information was located in a certain part of each cell. They tied the process of heredity to evolution, the process by which kinds of living things change in response to changing environments over time. At mid-century, they discovered the chemical mechanisms behind heredity.

Until the 1970s, geneticists concentrated on learning what genes were and how they worked. Such work continues today, shedding new light on how genes keep people healthy or contribute to diseases such as cancer. Indeed, some scientists today are engaged in the biggest gene-study project of all: the Human Genome Project, an attempt to read the coded message in each of a human's 100,000 genes.

In 1972, however, researchers began doing more than studying genes: they discovered how to change them. Working at first with microscopic life forms, they moved genes from one kind of living thing to another. "Genetic engineering" has created bacteria that churn out lifesaving drugs, plants that produce their own pesticides, and cattle that make human milk hormones. Doctors have even treated a human disease by altering genes.

Geneticists' research seldom attracted public attention in the early days of the science. Today, however, it makes headlines. People are growing more aware that in the century to come, the discoveries of geneticists and genetic engineers are likely to change society in major ways. They may determine who is sick and who is well, who gets jobs or health care and who does not. They could change the very meaning of being human.

The story of the great discoveries of genetics and genetic engineering is inspiring in itself. It shows men and women using patience and creativity to unravel one of the central mysteries of life. In addition, it offers hints about ways that power given by this new knowledge may be used—and perhaps misused—in the years ahead. This is an issue that deeply concerns us all.

Further Reading

The following are general books about genetics and genetic engineering.

Edelson, Edward. *Genetics and Heredity*. New York: Chelsea House, 1990. For young adults. Solid overview of genetics and the impact of heredity on human beings.

Genetics and Heredity. New York: Torstar, 1985. Well-illustrated overview of genetics, focusing on human beings.

Gonick, Larry, and Mark Wheelis. *The Cartoon Guide to Genetics*. New York: Harper and Row/Barnes and Noble, 1983. Scientifically accurate description of the basic concepts of genetics, presented in a humorous style.

Klein, Aaron E. *Threads of Life: Genetics from Aristotle to DNA*. Garden City, N.Y.: Natural History Press, 1970. For young adults. Describes the great discoveries and scientists of genetics in a clear and interesting way.

Swisher, Clarice. *Genetic Engineering*. San Diego: Lucent, 1996. For young adults. Good introduction to the topic.

Wingerson, Lois. *Mapping Our Genes: The Genome Project and the Future of Medicine*. New York: Penguin/Plume, 1991. Moving anecdotes describe the impact of inherited diseases and possible social effects of current genetic research.

NOTES

p . i x   "they [are] so much . . ." Quoted in Donald Dale Jackson. "Reunion of Identical Twins, Raised Apart, Reveals Some Astonishing Similarities," *Smithsonian*, October 1980, p. 50.

p . x   "We used to think . . ." Quoted in Leon Jaroff. "Happy Birthday, Double Helix." *Time*, March 15, 1993, p. 57.

Key to Icons in Boxed Features

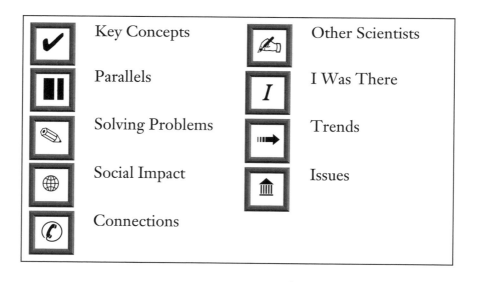

✔	Key Concepts	✍	Other Scientists
▮▮	Parallels	*I*	I Was There
✎	Solving Problems	▮▶	Trends
⊕	Social Impact	🏛	Issues
☎	Connections		

Revelations in a Garden

GREGOR MENDEL AND THE LAWS OF INHERITANCE

Gregor Mendel, an Austrian monk, discovered the basic rules govern-
ing the way living things pass on characteristics to their offspring.
(Courtesy National Library of Medicine)

In 1859, a British naturalist named Charles Darwin startled the scientific world, and a lot of the popular world, too. In a book called *On the Origin of Species*, Darwin claimed that species, or particular kinds of living things, slowly changed or evolved over time. Suppose, he said, that a member of a species was born a little different from others of its kind—one sparrow had a longer or shorter bill than other sparrows, for instance—and that difference helped it survive in its environment. That living thing would be more likely than others of its species to live long enough to have offspring. At least some of its offspring would inherit the useful characteristic and, in turn, would pass it on to their descendants. In time, creatures with the new characteristic would replace those that lacked it.

Darwin's theory of evolution shocked ordinary people because it contradicted the story of the creation of the world told in the

OTHER SCIENTISTS

INHERITED OR ACQUIRED?

Rather than accepting Charles Darwin's theory of evolution, many 19th-century scientists preferred the ideas of French naturalist Jean-Baptiste Lamarck (1744–1829). Lamarck believed that characteristics acquired *during* a living thing's lifetime could be passed on to its descendants. If drought forced giraffes to stretch their necks to reach leaves in tall trees in order to get enough to eat, for example, Lamarck said that their offspring would inherit longer necks. This suggested that environment could directly change heredity, a belief Darwin did not share. In the 20th century, when the laws of heredity discovered by Gregor Mendel were shown to provide a mechanism for evolution as Darwin defined it, Lamarck's theory was discarded.

British naturalist Charles Darwin explained how types of living things changed, or evolved, over time, but he did not understand the mechanism that allowed them to do so. Gregor Mendel's experiments with peas provided the first clue to this mystery. (Courtesy Edgar Fahs Smith Collection, Special Collections, Van Pelt-Dietrich Library, University of Pennsylvania)

Bible. Scientists had other objections to it. Some pointed out, for instance, that Darwin could not explain exactly how offspring inherited characteristics, or traits, from their parents. Darwin admitted that this question puzzled him.

Darwin never knew it, but while people were busy arguing about his theory, a quiet man in another country was carrying out experiments that would begin to solve the mystery of heredity.

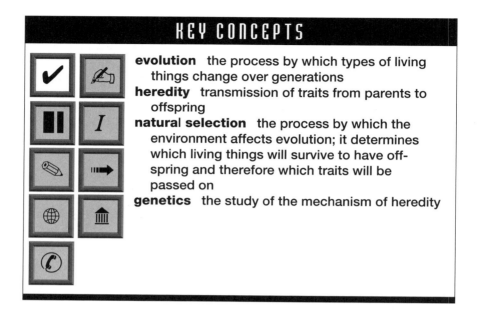

KEY CONCEPTS

evolution the process by which types of living things change over generations

heredity transmission of traits from parents to offspring

natural selection the process by which the environment affects evolution; it determines which living things will survive to have offspring and therefore which traits will be passed on

genetics the study of the mechanism of heredity

Ironically, in light of the fierce opposition of many churchmen to Darwin's ideas, the man was an Augustinian monk. His name was Gregor Mendel.

A Peasant Becomes a Scientist

The man who discovered the laws of heredity had not started life with the name of Gregor. He was born Johann Mendel in 1822 in the village of Heinzendorf, in a region called Moravia. At the time, Moravia was part of the empire of Austria-Hungary. It belongs to the Czech Republic today.

Johann's family were peasant farmers and gardeners, and he apparently inherited their love of growing things. His parish priest and village schoolteacher noticed that he was unusually intelligent, and they helped him get secondary schooling, something few peasant boys received. Mendel's father was seriously injured in an accident in 1838, however, and after that there was no more money to pay for school. Mendel managed to support himself long enough to start college courses, but the struggle to get enough money was so great that it made him ill.

One of Mendel's college professors suggested a solution for his problems. The professor pointed out that if Mendel joined the Augustinians, an order of monks whose main work was teaching, the order would pay for his education. In 1843, when he was 21 years old, Mendel took his professor's advice and joined the Augustinian monastery in the town of Brünn (now Brno, in the Czech Republic). The monastery required him to take a new name, and he chose Gregor.

Encouraged by the monks, Mendel became a substitute teacher in the local secondary school. To become a full-time teacher, however, he needed to pass an examination. The first time he tried, he failed. In 1851, therefore, the Augustinians sent Mendel to the University of Vienna to improve his education. He studied there for three years. Vitezslav Orel, a biographer of Mendel, says that at the university Mendel learned "all the basic . . . knowledge which made up the contemporary scientist's view of the world."

In his physics classes, Mendel learned that all the basic physical phenomena of nature were governed by a few relatively simple mathematical laws. The chief goal of science in Mendel's time was to discover similar laws behind more complex phenomena, such as weather and the behavior of living things. He also learned that all types of matter, regardless of how different they seemed, were made of the same kinds of fundamental particles. The basic units of physical matter were atoms, which combined to form molecules. The units that made up living things were microscopic bodies called cells.

In spite of all his studying, Mendel failed his teaching examination again in 1856. After that he continued to teach as a substitute, but he turned more and more to his first love, gardening. The Brünn monastery had a large garden and greenhouse, and the abbot (head of the monastery) gave Mendel part of each to use in any way he liked.

Generations of Peas

Mendel became curious about the way certain traits in plants were inherited, especially when plants with different characteristics were mated. Such a mating was called a cross, and the resulting offspring were known as hybrids. Hybrid offspring often showed the characteristics of both parents, but not always. Traits sometimes seemed to vanish, only to reappear in later generations. Mendel wondered what caused this and whether there was any pattern in the way it occurred.

He was hardly the first to wonder. People from earliest times had known that traits could be passed down from parents to offspring: human children, for instance, often resembled their parents. From the time humans began raising plants and animals, they tried to improve their stocks by deliberately mating those that had the most desirable characteristics, a process called breeding. Over time, breeding was often successful, but no one knew why it succeeded—or why it sometimes failed.

It was no surprise that people of Mendel's time did not understand heredity. They were just beginning to understand the process of reproduction. Biologists accepted the idea that most living things were the product of a male and a female parent, but many still argued about what role each gender played in the process. Mendel shared the view that both parents contributed equally to their offspring. Each provided a single cell: the father donated a sperm and the mother an egg. These two cells fused to make one cell, the fertilized egg. This then began dividing, eventually forming a new living thing. It was clear that these sex cells, the sperm and the eggs, must carry inherited information, but no one was sure how it got into them.

Mendel decided to do hybridization experiments using common edible, or garden, peas. Besides being easy to grow, peas had a number of traits in their seeds and plants that were easy to identify. Mendel chose seven traits to work with, including the height of the plants, the color of their seeds, and the shape of the seeds.

By putting pollen, which contained male (sperm) cells, from one plant onto the pistil, which led to the female (egg) cells, of another, Mendel mated plants that differed in particular characteristics. He then counted the number of offspring plants that showed each form of the characteristic he was testing. Afterward, he let these hybrid offspring, and later, their offspring, fertilize themselves. In self-fertilization, the sperm and the eggs came from the same parent. He continued this process for several generations, always counting the number of offspring with each form of the trait.

In planning and carrying out his experiments, Mendel did several things that no earlier researcher on heredity had done. First, instead of studying the whole appearance of the plants, he focused on just a few characteristics. He chose traits that existed in two forms that were easy to tell apart. Second, instead of examining just a few examples, Mendel grew and studied almost 30,000 pea plants over a period of eight years. He followed some plants through seven generations. Finally, instead of merely making generalizations about what happened to the plants, he counted the exact number that showed each trait. He then used mathematics to discover general rules about the way the characteristics were inherited. Mendel was one of the first to use statistics, the study and analysis of numerical information, in science.

Patterns of Inheritance

As Mendel tabulated the results of hundreds of crosses and self-fertilizations, he saw certain patterns appear. When he crossed tall plants with short ones, for instance, the resulting hybrid plants were always tall. There were no short or medium-sized ones. If he allowed the hybrid plants to self-fertilize, however, the shortness trait reappeared as if by magic: about one in every four of the second-generation plants was short. In a third generation produced by self-fertilization, the short plants always produced more short plants. One-third of the tall plants produced only tall plants.

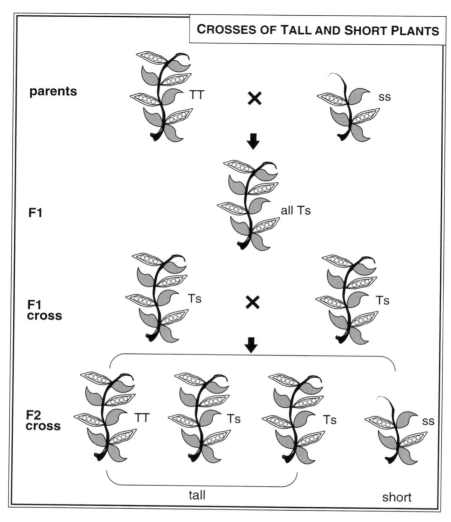

CROSSES OF TALL AND SHORT PLANTS

parents   TT   ×   ss

F1   all Ts

F1 cross   Ts   ×   Ts

F2 cross   TT   Ts   Ts   ss

tall   short

Gregor Mendel mated, or crossed, pea plants with different characteristics and studied their offspring. For instance, he mated purebred tall pea plants (tall plants that always gave tall offspring, shown here as TT) with purebred short plants (ss). All offspring in the first generation (F1) from this mating were tall, but they carried a hidden shortness "factor" from one parent as well as a tallness factor from the other (Ts). When those plants were self-fertilized to produce a second generation (F2), three out of four plants were tall. Mendel concluded that the short plants had inherited shortness factors from both parents (ss), and one out of the three tall plants had inherited tallness factors from both parents. The other two tall plants, like their parents, carried both a tallness and a shortness factor (Ts) and could pass either on to their offspring.

The other two-thirds produced both tall and short plants, again in the ratio of about 3 to 1. These results held through all later generations.

The same results appeared with all the other characteristics Mendel tested. One form of each trait proved to be about three times more common than the other in all generations after the first one. Mendel referred to the form of the characteristic that was most common as dominant, or controlling. He called the less common form recessive, meaning that it tended to recede or withdraw from view.

The relationship between dominant and recessive characteristics was not the only law of heredity that Mendel discovered. He also found that the traits he studied were inherited independently of each other. For instance, the pattern of inheritance for smooth and wrinkled seeds was the same, whether the seeds came from tall plants or short ones. It also did not matter which parent carried which trait—whether the male or the female plant was tall, for instance.

ISSUES

WERE MENDEL'S RESULTS "TOO GOOD TO BE TRUE?"

In 1936, a British statistician named Ronald Fisher claimed that Mendel or an assistant must have falsified his data. Fisher believed this because Mendel's results fit his theory more exactly than seemed statistically likely. Most modern studies, however, have acquitted Mendel of deliberate fraud. At most, in cases where the classification of a pea or a plant was in doubt (should a slightly dimpled seed be called smooth or wrinkled?), Mendel may have chosen the classification that fitted the results he expected to see.

Mendel concluded that each seed contained two "factors" that specified the form of each trait. The seed got one factor from the egg and one from the sperm. Since each of the plant parents would also have had two factors for the trait, Mendel concluded that each parent's pair of factors had to separate somehow during the formation of sex cells. If that did not happen, the offspring would inherit four factors, not two. If a parent was a hybrid, carrying two different factors for a trait, half of its sex cells would contain one kind of factor and the other half would contain the other. Chance would determine which factor a particular offspring received.

If both factors that an offspring inherited were the same, the offspring would show that form of the trait and would pass on only that form to its descendants. If a plant received two different factors, however, such as a tallness factor from one parent and a shortness factor from the other, it would show the form of the dominant factor. It could, however, pass on either the tallness or the shortness factor to its own descendants. This theory explained the 3:1 ratio between dominant and recessive traits that Mendel found.

Unappreciated Genius

Mendel wrote a paper describing his work in 1865. He addressed it mostly to plant breeders, but a farsighted comment that he made in the introduction suggests that he guessed his results might be important to a much wider audience. With a bit of pardonable pride he wrote:

> It requires indeed some courage to undertake a labor of such far-reaching extent; this appears, however, to be the only right way by which we can finally reach the solution of a question the importance of which cannot be overestimated in connection with the history of the evolution of organic forms [living things].

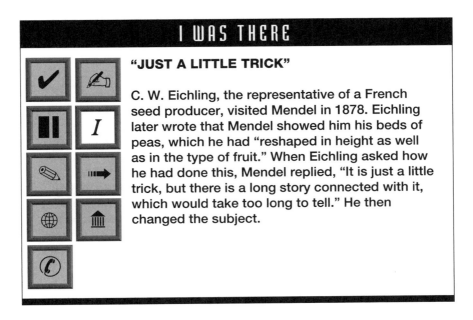

I WAS THERE

"JUST A LITTLE TRICK"

C. W. Eichling, the representative of a French seed producer, visited Mendel in 1878. Eichling later wrote that Mendel showed him his beds of peas, which he had "reshaped in height as well as in the type of fruit." When Eichling asked how he had done this, Mendel replied, "It is just a little trick, but there is a long story connected with it, which would take too long to tell." He then changed the subject.

Beyond this, Mendel never spoke of evolution directly, but he did know about Darwin's ideas. A friend of his wrote later that Mendel "was far from being an adversary of the Darwinian theory." However, Mendel felt that "there [was] still something lacking" in the theory. He may have realized that his own work made a good start toward supplying that something: a mechanism for the variation Darwin described.

Mendel's paper, "Experiments in Plant Hybridization," was published in a small scientific journal in 1866. No one paid much attention to it. Two years later Mendel was elected abbot of the Brünn monastery, and after that he was too busy to have much time for gardening.

Mendel never entirely gave up hope that someday his painstaking experiments would be appreciated. Shortly before his death in 1884, he told Friar Barina, a fellow monk, "My scientific work has brought me a great deal of satisfaction, and I am convinced that it will not be long before the whole world acknowledges it."

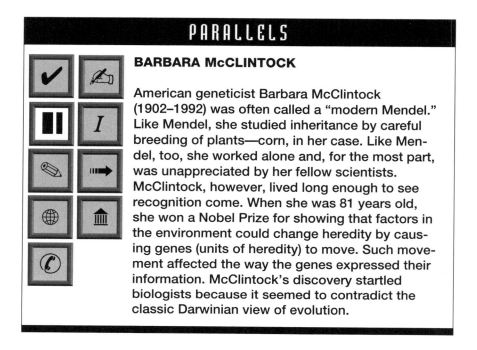

PARALLELS

BARBARA McCLINTOCK

American geneticist Barbara McClintock (1902–1992) was often called a "modern Mendel." Like Mendel, she studied inheritance by careful breeding of plants—corn, in her case. Like Mendel, too, she worked alone and, for the most part, was unappreciated by her fellow scientists. McClintock, however, lived long enough to see recognition come. When she was 81 years old, she won a Nobel Prize for showing that factors in the environment could change heredity by causing genes (units of heredity) to move. Such movement affected the way the genes expressed their information. McClintock's discovery startled biologists because it seemed to contradict the classic Darwinian view of evolution.

Mendel Rediscovered

The world did not get around to acknowledging Mendel for another 16 years. Then a Dutch scientist, Hugo de Vries, did some plant-breeding experiments that produced results basically identical to Mendel's. At the time he did this work, de Vries had never heard of Mendel. Before publishing his results, however, he searched the scientific literature to find out if anyone had done work similar to his, and he came upon a copy of Mendel's paper. In his own paper, which he published in 1900, de Vries wrote that his experiments had caused him to

> conclude that the law of segregation of hybrids in the plant kingdom, which Mendel established for peas, has a very general application and a fundamental significance for the study of the units out of which the specific characters [traits] are compounded.

By a startling coincidence, two other researchers, Carl Correns in Germany and Erich von Tschermak in Austria, rediscovered Mendel's work in the same year de Vries did. They worked independently of de Vries and each other. Like de Vries, they mentioned Mendel's work in papers that described their own plant-breeding experiments.

It was a fourth researcher, William Bateson, who really brought Mendel's name to the attention of the scientific community, however. Bateson, a British zoologist (scientist who studies animals), was traveling to London one day in May 1900 to give a speech about heredity to a meeting of the Royal Horticultural (plant-breeding) Society. He brought several papers to read on the train, and one of them happened to be a reprint of Mendel's paper.

Bateson was interested in the way heredity might relate to Charles Darwin's ideas of evolution and natural selection. Darwin had proposed that just as a plant or animal breeder selected living things with the most desirable characteristics to mate, so nature, in effect, selected living things with characteristics that suited a

OTHER SCIENTISTS

DE VRIES AND MUTATIONS

Hugo de Vries introduced the important concept of changes, or mutations, in particular inherited characteristics. In 1886, de Vries noticed that in a field of wildflowers called evening primroses, several flowers were different from the rest. When he bred these, they produced more offspring like themselves. De Vries maintained that evolution occurred through spontaneous, inheritable changes like this. Mutations later would be traced to changes in genes.

particular environment by making those living things more likely to produce offspring. This was how evolution took place.

Bateson agreed with most of Darwin's ideas. Still, like Mendel himself, he felt that "something was lacking" in the mechanism of Darwin's theory. Bateson's son, Gregory, wrote later that his father believed that

> natural selection could not be the only determinant of the direction of evolutionary change and that the genesis of variation could not be a random matter. He therefore set out to demonstrate regularity and "lawfulness" among the phenomena of variability.

When Bateson read Mendel's paper, he felt he had found the "lawfulness" he had been seeking. He rewrote his speech for the

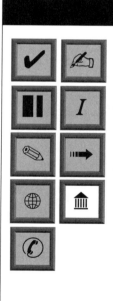

ISSUES

MENDELISTS AND BIOMETRICIANS

Mendel, de Vries, and Bateson thought of natural selection in terms of distinct changes in traits. Darwin, on the other hand, had believed that changes in species occurred through gradual, continuous variation in inherited traits. In the early 20th century, biologists who sided with Darwin in this matter called themselves biometricians because they measured traits that had a varying aspect. Both Mendelists and biometricians could offer examples to support their ideas: some traits do show gradual change, while others appear in distinctly different forms. The conflict between these two viewpoints was resolved only in the 1920s, when geneticists discovered that many traits are controlled by more than one gene. A change in a single gene, therefore, may cause only a slight variation in the trait. Changes in multiple genes can produce the appearance of continuous variation.

Horticultural Society to include a description of Mendel's work, saying that it would "certainly play a conspicuous part in all future discussions of evolutionary problems." He later helped to translate Mendel's paper from its original German into English. In fact, Bateson became a missionary for Mendel's ideas, describing them to everyone he met in his work.

Birth of a Science

Bateson had a reputation in the scientific community that Mendel had never had. This helped him reach a wider audience than Mendel had been able to do. Bateson's efforts were also successful because the times had changed. By the turn of the century, most scientists had accepted the basic idea of evolution. They therefore wanted to know about a possible mechanism by which evolution and natural selection might take place. In addition, improved microscopes had helped biologists learn more about cells and the reproductive process than had been known in Mendel's time. Scientists had seen a sperm and an egg joining, for instance. This new knowledge made acceptance of Mendel's ideas easier.

Bateson realized that Mendel's laws could become the foundation of a new science. In 1906 he coined the term *genetics* to describe that science. Genetics, he said, was

> The elucidation [explanation] of the phenomena of heredity and variation: in other words, . . . the physiology of Descent, with implied bearing on the theoretical problems of the evolutionist . . . and application to the practical problems of the breeders, whether of animals or plants.

Three years later, replacing Mendel's vague term *factor*, Danish biologist Wilhelm Johansson proposed that the unit of heredity—the information that produced one inherited trait—be called a gene. The term was kept even after scientists discovered that some traits are influenced by more than one gene.

SOCIAL IMPACT

GALTON AND EUGENICS

Many people in the late 19th century became interested in human heredity because of the writings of Francis Galton (1822–1911), a cousin of Charles Darwin. In a book called *Hereditary Genius*, published in 1869, Galton claimed to show that intelligence was inherited in the same way as physical traits. He coined the term *eugenics*, meaning "well born," to represent the idea that people with desirable traits such as intelligence should be encouraged to have children, whereas those with undesirable traits should be discouraged. Several groups in the 20th century, notably the Nazis in Germany in the 1930s and early 1940s, tried to impose eugenics by force. They sterilized or even killed people whom they considered genetically undesirable. In recent years, as scientists have gained the power to alter genes, fears of a new kind of eugenics have appeared.

Spurred on by the interest of evolutionists in the Mendelian theory, of plant and animal breeders in its practical uses, and of students of human heredity in its social implications, the newborn field of genetics grew quickly. Geneticists set about trying to solve the chief puzzle left unanswered by Mendel's work: what physical form genes took.

Chronology of the Birth of Genetics

1822   Johann Mendel born in Heinzendorf, Moravia
1843   Joins Augustinian monastery in Brünn and takes the name of Gregor
1851–53   Studies science at University of Vienna

1858–64 Experiments with pea plants in monastery garden; discovers laws of heredity
1859 Charles Darwin's *On the Origin of Species* published
1866 Mendel publishes paper about experiments
1868 Elected abbot of Brünn monastery; ends garden experiments
1869 Francis Galton claims that human intelligence is inherited
1884 Mendel dies
1900 Mendel's work rediscovered
1906 William Bateson coins term *genetics* to name new science based on Mendel's work

Further Reading

Klein, Aaron E. *Threads of Life*. Garden City, N.Y.: Natural History Press, 1970. For young adults. Contains an excellent chapter on Mendel.

Mendel, Gregor. "Experiments in Plant Hybridization." In Cedric I. Davern, ed., *Readings from Scientific American: Genetics*. San Francisco: W. H. Freeman, 1981. Mendel's original paper, translated into English. Difficult reading.

MendelWeb. World Wide Web: http://www.stg.brown.edu/MendelWeb/home.html. Contains information about Mendel, the text of his paper in English and German, and discussion of his work.

Miller, Julie Ann. "Mendel's Peas: A Matter of Genius or of Guile?" *Science News*, February 18, 1984. Discusses accusations that Mendel's work was "too good to be true."

Orel, Vitezslav. *Mendel*. Oxford and New York: Oxford University Press, 1984. Short biography of Mendel.

Schwartz, Joseph. *The Creative Moment*. New York: HarperCollins, 1992. Chapter 4 contains interesting material on the background of genetics and, especially, eugenics.

Seidler, Ned, and Rick Gore. "Seven Giants Who Led the Way." *National Geographic*, September 1976. Article on major early discoveries in biology includes section on Mendel.

NOTES

p. 5   "all the basic . . ." Vitezslav Orel. *Mendel* (Oxford: Oxford University Press, 1984), p. 129.

p. 10   "It requires indeed . . ." Quoted in Robert B. Downs. *Landmarks in Science* (Littleton, Colo.: Libraries Unlimited, 1982), p. 245.

p. 11   "reshaped in height . . . ," "It is just . . ." Quoted in Orel, p. 90.

p. 11   "was far from being an adversary . . ." Quoted in Orel, p. 71.

p. 11   "there [was] still something lacking." Quoted in Orel, p. 71.

p. 11   "My scientific work . . ." Quoted in Orel, p. 93.

p. 12   "conclude that the law . . ." Quoted in N. A. Tiley. *Discovering DNA* (New York: Van Nostrand Reinhold, 1983), p. 44.

p. 14   "natural selection could not be . . ." Quoted in Tiley, p. 46.

p. 15   "certainly play a conspicuous part . . ." Quoted in Aaron Klein. *Threads of Life* (Garden City, N.Y.: Natural History Press, 1970), p. 94.

p. 15   "The elucidation . . ." Quoted in R. C. Olby, et al., eds. *Companion to the History of Modern Science* (London: Routledge, 1990), p. 533.

2

The Fly Room

THOMAS HUNT MORGAN AND THE FIRST GENE MAPS

Thomas Hunt Morgan and his students in Columbia University's "Fly Room" used fruit flies to show how Mendel's rules of heredity operated in cells. (Courtesy National Library of Medicine)

The smell was unique: the sweet-sour odor of rotting bananas greeted visitors to Columbia University's famous "Fly Room" when they were still many doors away from their destination. The sounds were just as strange, made by the wings of thousands of tiny fruit flies buzzing against the glass of their half-pint milk bottles. Larval flies, the bottles' quieter residents, developed into adults while clinging to strips of paper torn from old letters sent to the Fly Room's chief scientist, Thomas Hunt Morgan.

The discoveries made in the Fly Room were unique, too. Morgan and his brilliant students and coworkers not only proved that Gregor Mendel's ideas had been right but linked Mendel's "factors" to a particular part of living cells. They found explanations for several situations in which Mendel's laws did *not* seem to hold. They discovered how genes determine whether a living thing will be male or female. And, finally, they began to define what genes are and make maps showing how they are arranged. These creative researchers made the new field of genetics a true experimental science.

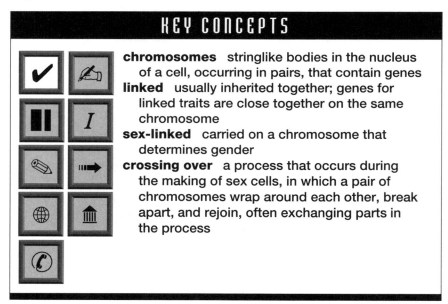

KEY CONCEPTS

chromosomes stringlike bodies in the nucleus of a cell, occurring in pairs, that contain genes

linked usually inherited together; genes for linked traits are close together on the same chromosome

sex-linked carried on a chromosome that determines gender

crossing over a process that occurs during the making of sex cells, in which a pair of chromosomes wrap around each other, break apart, and rejoin, often exchanging parts in the process

A Place for Genes

Attempts to find a physical basis for heredity began long before the smell of decaying bananas started wafting out of Columbia's windows. In 1875 a German scientist, Walther Flemming, found that the central part, or nucleus, of cells contained a material that could be stained with a bright dye. He named it chromatin, from a Greek word meaning "color." Just before a cell divided to make

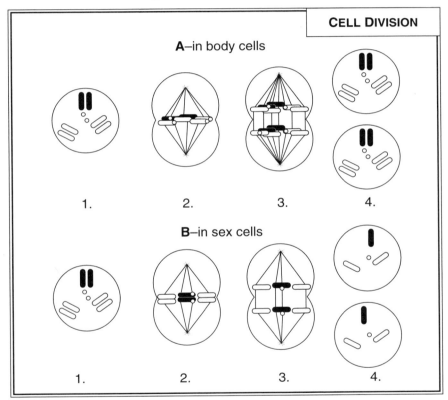

CELL DIVISION

A–in body cells

1.   2.   3.   4.

B–in sex cells

1.   2.   3.   4.

A. Chromosomes exist in pairs (1). When a body cell gets ready to divide, the pairs line up in the center of the cell (2), then separate (3). Each chromosome makes a copy of itself. After the cell divides, each of the two "daughter cells" has a set of chromosomes just like that of the parent. B. When the sex cells form, something different happens. The chromosomes line up (2) and separate (3), but they do not duplicate themselves. As a result, each sex cell receives only one member of each pair of chromosomes. It therefore has half as many chromosomes as a body cell (4).

two daughter cells, Flemming saw the chromatin form into string-like bodies that he called chromosomes.

American geneticist Walter Sutton was one of the first scientists to propose a connection between Mendel's factors and chromosomes. Sutton made this suggestion in 1902, when he was just 25 years old. He pointed out that the chromosomes grouped themselves into similar-looking pairs. Somehow the pairs duplicated themselves, and then, as the cell grew longer and began to split, they pulled apart. When the daughter cells formed, each ended up with a set of chromosomes just like those that had been in the parent cell.

There was one exception to this behavior: the formation of sex cells, the sperm and the egg. When those cells were created, Sutton saw that the pairs of chromosomes split, but they did not duplicate themselves. Each sex cell, therefore, ended up with only half the normal number of chromosomes for that kind of living thing. (Different kinds of living things have different numbers of chromosomes. Humans have 46, for instance.) When the sperm and egg joined, the resulting fertilized egg again had the full number of chromosomes—half from the male and half from the female parent.

All this was exactly what Mendel had said must happen with his factors. It seemed likely, therefore, that the factors were part of the chromosomes. It was clear, though, that each chromosome had to carry more than one factor. No living thing had enough chromosomes to represent the thousands of traits it possessed.

From Civil War to Fruit Flies

Some geneticists—scientists who studied genetics—believed Sutton's chromosome theory, while others doubted it. Thomas Hunt Morgan was one of the doubters. For one thing, he pointed out, all cells in a living thing's body contained identical chromosomes. Nonetheless, muscle cells, for instance, were very different from nerve cells or blood cells. To Morgan, this suggested that inherited information must be somewhere else in the cell.

Morgan came from a Kentucky family that had played a thrilling part in the Civil War. His uncle, John Hunt Morgan, had been called "The Thunderbolt of the Confederacy." He had staged daring raids into Union territory and escaped from a Union prison before being killed in 1864. Thomas Hunt Morgan was born at the family home in Lexington two years later, in the same year Gregor Mendel published his paper on peas.

Unlike most of his family, Thomas Morgan was more interested in science than in Southern history. After two years at the State College of Kentucky, he went to Johns Hopkins, a university in Baltimore, Maryland. Johns Hopkins was one of the best places in the country to learn biology. Morgan focused on embryology, the study of how living things develop before birth.

I WAS THERE

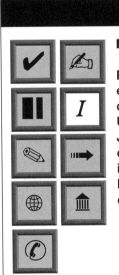

MORGAN SEES THE LIGHT

For years, Thomas Morgan doubted the theory of evolution and natural selection as well as the chromosome theory. When Morgan visited Oxford University in England in 1922, however, biologist Julian Huxley, grandson of one of Darwin's strongest supporters, showed him part of the university's insect collection. This included a display of unrelated butterflies with similar coloration, a clear effect of natural selection. Huxley later wrote,

> When I went back to fetch him for a luncheon, I could hardly prevail on him to move. "This is extraordinary! I just didn't know things like this existed!" [Morgan exclaimed.] . . . It was, I am proud to believe, the occasion of his conversion to a belief in adaptation and the efficacy [effectiveness] of natural selection in producing it.

Morgan received his doctorate in 1890. He then began teaching biology at Bryn Mawr, a women's college near Philadelphia. One of the students he met there was Lilian Vaughan Sampson, who became his wife in 1904. Just after his marriage, Morgan moved to Columbia University in New York City.

Morgan and his students at Columbia worked with a number of different animals, but the most useful proved to be the fruit fly, or vinegar fly. This common pest insect had hitchhiked to the United States from Central America on banana shipments in the 1870s. The quarter-inch-long flies were fine subjects for genetics experiments. They were easy to catch—just put a piece of rotting banana on the sill of an open window—and cheap to feed. Thousands could be kept in even a small laboratory. Mendel had had to wait a year for each new generation of his pea plants, but fruit flies produced a new generation every 10 days or so. Each female laid hundreds of eggs, so it was easy to study large numbers of offspring from the same mating.

Genes Linked Together

Morgan tried to produce mutations in his fruit flies by exposing them to X rays or radium. At first, nothing unusual happened. "There's two years' work wasted," Morgan told a friend early in 1910.

Morgan's feelings changed, though, in May of the same year. One day he was peering at some of the tiny flies (anesthetized with ether so they would hold still) through a magnifying lens when he noticed that one of them, a male, had white eyes. The usual color of fruit fly eyes is red. Morgan knew he had found a mutant, a creature that showed a spontaneous change in an inherited characteristic.

Morgan carefully picked up the white-eyed fly and put it in a clean milk bottle along with a normal, red-eyed female. Ten days later, 1,240 new flies hatched in the bottle. All had red eyes, as would be expected if the gene for red eye color were dominant over the one for white. When these flies were mated to each other, the next generation showed a classic Mendelian inheritance pattern, with three-fourths of the flies having red eyes and one-fourth having white. There was one fascinating difference, though: all the white-eyed flies were male. The inheritance of the traits Mendel had studied was not affected by sex, but this apparently was not always true in fruit flies. Morgan concluded that the gene for red or white (absence of red) eye color must be inherited with, or linked to, the gene that determined sex.

In 1905 Edmund Wilson and Nettie Stevens had noted that, although the chromosomes in a pair were usually alike, in many animals—including fruit flies—there was an exception in the male. One chromosome in one pair in males was smaller than the other and had a different shape. The scientists called this strange little chromosome the Y chromosome. Females inherited two normal-looking chromosomes called X chromosomes. Males, instead, inherited an X from their mothers and a Y from their fathers. The presence of the Y chromosome somehow seemed to cause maleness. This is true in humans, too.

Morgan and his students soon found several other mutations that affected eye color. One produced pink eyes, while another resulted in vermilion, or dark red, eyes. The vermilion form, like the white form, was sex-linked, or sex-limited as Morgan then called it, but the pink was not. Clearly several genes could affect eye color, but, like the traits Mendel had studied, they did not usually interact with each other. They apparently were in different parts of what Morgan called the hereditary mechanism.

In 1911 Morgan concluded that a sex gene and the eye color genes linked to it must both be on the X chromosome. He could think of no other reason why they would be inherited together. Female flies in the first generation resulting from the mating of the red-eyed female and the white-eyed male, with their two X chromosomes, carried both a red-eye gene and a white-eye gene. (Since the red-eye gene was dominant, they all had red eyes.) They passed one gene to half their offspring and the other gene to the other half. Males in the first generation, on the other hand, could inherit an X chromosome only from their red-eyed mother.

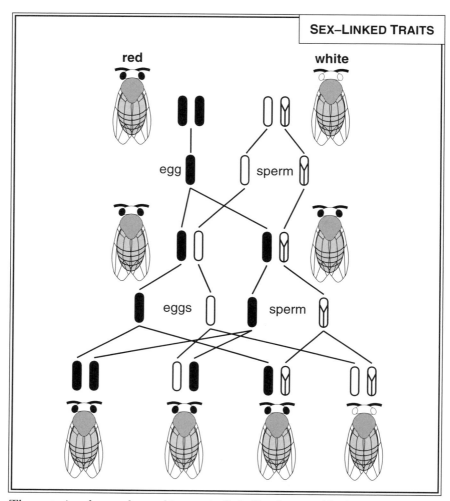

SEX–LINKED TRAITS

red

white

egg

sperm

eggs

sperm

The mutation that produces white eyes in fruit flies shows itself only in males. Thomas Hunt Morgan determined that it is sex-linked, or carried on the same chromosome as genes that determine gender. These drawings show the result of a mating between a red-eyed female fly (red is the normal color) and a white-eyed male fly. The oval with the Y inside is a Y chromosome, found only in males. The plain white and black ovals are X chromosomes. Flies with two X chromosomes are females, while those with an X and a Y chromosome are males. Female flies will always have red eyes because the gene for red eyes is dominant, but they may carry the white-eye gene on one of their X chromosomes. Males will have red or white eyes, depending on whether they inherit an X chromosome carrying the red-eye gene (black oval) or one carrying the white-eye gene (white oval) from their mothers. The lines show matings between flies carrying different genes.

In the second generation, half the females inherited two red-eye genes and half a red- and a white-eye gene. Half the males received a red-eye gene on their single X chromosome, and half received a white-eye gene, inherited from mothers who carried both forms. The males that inherited the single white-eye gene would show white eyes. Like their grandfathers, they could pass this gene on to their daughters but not their sons.

The fruit fly research was so exciting that most of the people in Morgan's laboratory soon became engaged in it, and Columbia's Fly Room was born. Alfred Sturtevant, a student of Morgan's who became a lifelong friend, wrote later,

SOCIAL IMPACT

A "ROYAL" DISEASE LEADS TO REVOLUTION

Certain human diseases are inherited, and some are sex linked. One of the most striking is a blood disease called hemophilia. The recessive gene that causes the disease, like the white-eye gene Morgan studied in his fruit flies, is on the X chromosome. Females carry the gene but, because they usually have one normal X chromosome, rarely show the disease. People with hemophilia lack a substance that makes the blood clot, so they bleed easily from even small injuries. Blood seeps into their joints and tissues, causing great pain.

The family of Britain's 19th-century queen Victoria carried the hemophilia gene, and her daughters passed it on to other royal families of Europe through their marriages. Victoria's granddaughter, Alexandra, married the ruler of Russia in the early 20th century and had a son with hemophilia. A monk named Rasputin seemed to help the boy, and she rewarded him with great power. Some historians feel that the Russians' dislike of Rasputin helped to bring about the Russian Revolution in 1917.

There can have been few times and places in scientific laboratories with such an atmosphere of excitement and such a record of sustained enthusiasm. . . . This group worked as a unit. Each carried out his own experiments but each knew exactly what the others were doing, and each new result was freely discussed.

By 1912, Morgan and his coworkers had identified 40 different mutations in their flies. The mutations affected not only eye color but coloration and shape of wings, body, legs, and other parts of the fly. Linkage clustered them into four groups—the same number as the number of chromosome pairs in the fruit fly. This observation helped to convince Morgan that genes were indeed carried on chromosomes. Additional evidence came from the fact that one pair of fruit fly chromosomes was smaller than the others, and one of the linkage groups also contained far fewer mutations than the others. The number of genes in each linkage group thus appeared to be related to the length of the chromosome pair that probably carried them.

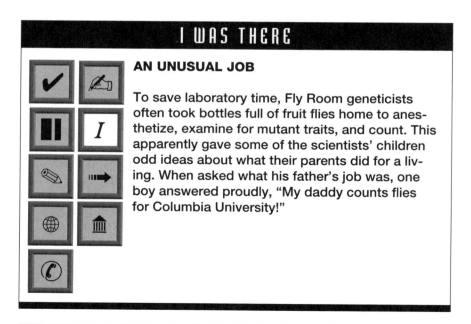

I WAS THERE

AN UNUSUAL JOB

To save laboratory time, Fly Room geneticists often took bottles full of fruit flies home to anesthetize, examine for mutant traits, and count. This apparently gave some of the scientists' children odd ideas about what their parents did for a living. When asked what his father's job was, one boy answered proudly, "My daddy counts flies for Columbia University!"

SOLVING PROBLEMS

DETERMINING LINKAGE

When Morgan and his students found a new fly mutant, they first bred it with a normal fly. They then mated its offspring with each other until they got a stock of flies that showed the mutation dependably. Male flies with the new mutation were next mated with females that carried mutations known to be on particular chromosomes. These known mutations served as markers for those chromosomes; white eye, for instance, became a marker for the X chromosome. The group could then see which of these marker traits the new mutation was inherited with. That showed which chromosome contained the gene for the new mutation.

Morgan's research also showed that Mendel had been right in saying that the characteristics he studied did not affect each other's inheritance—but the monk had also been very lucky. Mendel had happened to pick traits that were carried on different chromosomes of the pea plant (it has seven pairs), so they were not linked. In many other cases, Morgan wrote in 1911, "Instead of random segregation in Mendel's sense we find 'associations of factors' that are located near together in the chromosomes."

Crossing Over and Chromosome Maps

Studying a mutation they called miniature wing, Morgan's group uncovered another puzzle. This mutation, like white eye, was sex-linked, so the two were usually inherited together—but not always. A look at fly chromosomes under a microscope suggested a possible reason. Danish biologist F. A. Janssen had shown in 1909 that just before pairs of chromosomes divided while forming sex cells, they twisted around each other. Morgan suspected that

CROSSING OVER

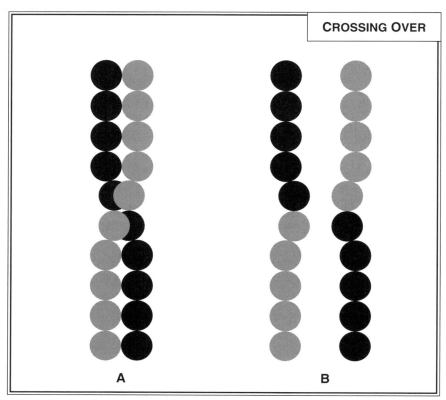

A   B

Pairs of chromosomes separate when eggs and sperm are formed, leaving each sex cell with half as many chromosomes as a body cell. Before they separate, the chromosomes in each pair wrap around each other. Often the chromosomes break during this process. When they rejoin, part of one chromosome becomes stuck onto part of the other, resulting in a chromosome that contains genes from both members of the original pair. This process is called crossing over or recombination.

when the chromosomes separated again, both chromosomes broke into pieces. The broken pieces rejoined to form whole chromosomes, but in the process, part of one chromosome often stuck onto part of another. All the genes on the broken piece therefore moved from the first chromosome to the second. Morgan called this process crossing over. It was later also known as recombination.

Morgan pictured genes as being lined up along a chromosome like beads on a string. He guessed that linked genes that often became separated by crossing over, such as those for miniature wing and white eye, were far apart on their original chromosome. Almost any break, no matter where it occurred, would separate them. Linked genes that seldom became separated, on the other hand, were probably close together. Only if a break occurred in the small space between them would they be forced apart. Hermann Müller, a student of Morgan's, later wrote:

> Morgan's evidence for crossing over and his suggestion that genes further apart cross over more frequently was a thunderclap: hardly second to the discovery of Mendelism, which ushered in that storm that has given nourishment to all our modern genetics.

Another of Morgan's students, Alfred Sturtevant, was just 21 years old and still an undergraduate when he made another intuitive leap. As he wrote later,

> In the latter part of 1911 . . . I suddenly realized that the variations in strength of linkage, already attributed by Morgan to differences in the spatial separation of the genes, offered the possibility of determining sequences in the linear dimension of a chromosome. I went home and spent most of the night (to the neglect of my undergraduate homework) in producing the first chromosome map.

Sturtevant and others in the Fly Room went on to make other maps of fruit fly chromosomes, placing on them the mutations they knew about. Even though they could not see actual genes and indeed were not even sure what physical form genes took, they determined the genes' relative distance apart on the chromosomes with an accuracy that still held up decades later.

Morgan summed up the work of the Fly Room in a book called *The Mechanism of Mendelian Heredity*, which was published in 1915. It both proved that Mendel's results were basically correct and explained cases in which they did not apply. It offered the best evidence yet that genes were part of chromosomes. It thus tied

CONNECTIONS

FRUIT FLIES AND "HOMEO BOX" GENES

Fruit flies are still vital tools of genetic research. Experiments with these insects have recently shed important light on a subject that intrigued Thomas Hunt Morgan: how living things develop before birth. In the mid-1980s, two scientists independently discovered a stretch of genetic material (DNA—see Chapter 3) that appeared in several genes that control fruit fly development. Mutations in these genes produce such monsters as a fly with legs growing out of its head. The genes are called homeotic genes, from a Greek word meaning "similar," because the misplaced parts produced by such mutations are similar to normal body parts. This same piece of DNA was later found in the homeotic genes of living things ranging from sea urchins to humans. It has the power to stick to other genes' DNA. Scientists call this special piece of DNA the "homeo box." They believe that it attaches to and thereby controls other genes, turning them on and off during development.

theories derived from breeding experiments to what could be seen under a microscope.

Morgan was awarded the Nobel Prize in Physiology or Medicine in 1933. He told the Nobel committee, however, that he was too busy to go to Sweden to collect the prize that year. (He stopped by to pick it up a year later.) For one thing, he was excitedly following the work of scientists who had just discovered that cells in the immature (larval) fruit fly's salivary glands (glands in the mouth that make saliva) contain giant chromosomes. These chromosomes were 2,000 times bigger than the normal ones, which had been too small to see in any detail even with a good microscope.

The giant salivary gland chromosomes were striped with light and dark bands that were easy to see and count. By watching what happened to these bands, geneticists could directly observe crossing over and other behavior that Morgan and his coworkers had inferred from their breeding experiments. They could check the group's gene maps. To Morgan's delight, studies of the new chromosomes fully supported his earlier work.

Morgan's "Greatest Discoveries"

Important as Morgan's achievements in genetics were, a scientist friend once said that Morgan's greatest discoveries were his students. Morgan had a knack for recognizing, drawing to him, and encouraging brilliant young people. Three of his early students, Alfred Sturtevant, Calvin Bridges, and Hermann Müller, had distinguished careers as geneticists, and one, Müller, went on to win his own Nobel Prize. The prize, given in 1946, was for

OTHER SCIENTISTS

HERMANN MÜLLER

Hermann Müller (1890–1967) was ahead of his time in his ideas about what a gene was. In 1921 he predicted that genes would prove to be very tiny particles in cells that, in spite of their size, would have a complex structure. He also predicted that humans eventually would become able to guide their own evolution. He suggested establishing sperm banks so that women could choose sperm from men with especially desirable characteristics to produce their children.

SOCIAL IMPACT

RADIATION AND HUMAN MUTATIONS

After X rays and other forms of high-energy radiation became widely used in the early 20th century, it eventually became obvious that radiation caused an increase in mutations in human beings as well as fruit flies. People exposed to radiation often later developed cancer because of genetic damage that the radiation had caused. Their children also were likely to suffer from birth defects. The genetic effects of radiation were most tragically shown in the people who survived the atomic bombing of Hiroshima and Nagasaki in Japan at the end of World War II.

Müller's demonstration in 1927 that exposing fruit flies to X rays greatly increased the number of mutations in their offspring. Like Hugo de Vries, Müller believed that mutations were the root of evolution. Being able to produce and study them, therefore, was vital to genetics.

A later student of Morgan's, George Beadle, was also a Nobel winner. Beadle studied under Morgan at the California Institute of Technology (Caltech) in Pasadena, where Morgan spent the later years of his research career. Working with Edward L. Tatum at Stanford University, Beadle used X rays to produce mutations in a type of bread mold called *Neurospora*. Beadle and Tatum showed in 1941 that all these mutations affected cell substances called proteins. This led to the idea that all genes produced traits through ordering the making of different proteins. Each gene carried the instructions for making one protein. Through discoveries like this, Beadle and other students of Thomas Hunt Morgan transformed genetics from a study of organisms and cells to a study of the chemistry and physics that took place within those cells.

Chronology of Genetic Linkage and the First Chromosome Maps

1866	Thomas Hunt Morgan born in Lexington, Kentucky
1875	Walther Flemming discovers chromosomes
1902	Walter Sutton suggests that Mendel's factors are located on chromosomes
1904	Morgan begins work at Columbia University
1905	Edmund Wilson and Nettie Stevens discover difference in sex (X and Y) chromosomes
1910	Morgan discovers white-eyed fruit fly mutant
1911	Shows that the white-eye gene must be on the X chromosome; shows that genes that are linked, or inherited together, must be on the same chromosome; shows that linked genes can become separated during crossing over Alfred Sturtevant uses linkage studies to make first chromosome map
1915	Morgan's book, The Mechanism of Mendelian Heredity, summarizes research of Fly Room
1927	Hermann Muller shows that X rays greatly increase mutations in fruit flies
1928	Morgan moves to California Institute of Technology
1933	Wins Nobel Prize in Physiology or Medicine Giant chromosomes found in fruit fly salivary glands
1941	George Beadle and Edward Tatum show that each gene carries the information for making one protein
1945	Morgan dies

Further Reading

Klein, Aaron E. *Threads of Life*. Garden City, N.Y.: Natural History Press, 1970. For young adults. Contains an excellent chapter on Morgan.

Reingold, Nathan and Ida H. *Science in America: A Documentary History 1900–1939*. Chicago: University of Chicago Press, 1981. Includes summaries of genetic research in Morgan's time and correspondence between Morgan and other scientists.

Seidler, Ned, and Rick Gore. "Seven Giants Who Led the Way." *National Geographic*, September 1976. Article on major early discoveries in biology includes section on Morgan.

Sherrow, Victoria. *Great Scientists*. New York: Facts On File, 1992. For young adults. Includes a chapter on Morgan.

Shine, Ian, and Sylvia Wrobel. *Thomas Hunt Morgan: Pioneer of Genetics*. Lexington: University Press of Kentucky, 1976. Biography of Morgan.

NOTES

p. 23   "When I went back . . ." Quoted in Ian Shine and Sylvia Wrobel. *Thomas Hunt Morgan: Pioneer of Genetics* (Lexington: University of Kentucky, 1976), p. 57.

p. 24   "There's two years' work . . ." Quoted in Shine and Wrobel, p. 62.

p. 28   "There can have been few . . ." Quoted in Victoria Sherrow. *Great Scientists* (New York: Facts On File, 1992), p. 9.

p. 28   "This group worked . . ." Quoted in Shine and Wrobel, p. 83.

p. 28   "My daddy counts flies . . ." Quoted in Shine and Wrobel, p. 72.

p. 29   "Instead of random segregation . . ." Quoted in Shine and Wrobel, p. 78.

p. 31   "Morgan's evidence . . ." Quoted in Shine and Wrobel, p. 92.

p. 31   "In the latter part of 1911 . . ." Quoted in Shine and Wrobel, pp. 74–75.

3

The Code of Life

JAMES WATSON, FRANCIS CRICK, AND
THE STRUCTURE OF DNA

Francis Crick (left) and James Watson (right) worked out the structure of DNA, the molecule that carries hereditary information, mostly by talking as they sat in their office or strolled through England's Cambridge University. (Courtesy Cold Spring Harbor Laboratory)

The first clue about the chemical nature of genes came from what seemed like a magic trick. The "trick" used a kind of bacteria called pneumococcus. One form of these bacteria caused pneumonia, a serious lung disease. Another could not cause disease. In 1944 an American scientist named Oswald Avery and his coworkers turned the harmless form into the disease-causing one by adding to it a chemical called deoxyribonucleic acid, or DNA, that had been extracted from the disease-causing form. The descendants of the transformed bacteria also could cause disease, just as if they had inherited a gene that allowed them to do so.

KEY CONCEPTS

amino acid a simple cell chemical containing carbon, hydrogen, oxygen, and nitrogen; 20 kinds of amino acids can combine to form proteins

bacteriophage one of several kinds of viruses that infect and kill bacteria

bacterium (plural **bacteria**) a simple, single-celled organism

base one of four types of small molecules attached to the "backbone" of a nucleic acid; a gene's information is carried in the sequence of its bases

DNA deoxyribonucleic acid, the type of nucleic acid that carries genetic information in most living things

genetic code the code that allows DNA instructions to be translated into proteins

genome the complete collection of genes in a living thing

protein a complex cell chemical containing one or more of 20 kinds of amino acids; proteins give cells their structure and control chemical reactions in cells

virus a combination of nucleic acid and protein that can enter cells and use their machinery to make copies of itself, sometimes causing disease

THE CODE OF LIFE

Nucleic Acid or Protein?

Scientists had known about DNA for almost a century before Avery's experiment. A Swiss chemist, Johann Miescher, first found this clear, sticky chemical in the nucleus of cells in 1869, three years after Mendel's groundbreaking paper was published. Miescher called the substance nuclein, but the name was later changed to nucleic acid. Neither Miescher nor most of the scientists who followed him dreamed that nucleic acid was connected with heredity.

By the 1930s, most geneticists agreed that a gene must be some sort of complex chemical. Nucleic acids and proteins are the only two such chemicals in chromosomes. Until the time of Oswald Avery's bacteria-transforming experiment, most geneticists thought that genes would turn out to be protein. They did not believe that nucleic acids (DNA and a related chemical, ribonucleic acid or RNA) had a complicated enough structure to carry genetic information. Proteins, on the other hand, were clearly quite complex. Twenty different kinds of small "building-block" molecules, called amino acids, could contribute to making a single protein molecule. Protein molecules were strings of amino acid units, often hundreds of them, folded in complicated ways.

Avery showed, though, that the "magic" in his transforming trick came from pure DNA, with all protein removed. Further evidence to support the idea that genes were made of DNA came in 1952, when Alfred Hershey and Martha Chase showed that the material that a virus called a bacteriophage ("bacteria-eater") injected into bacteria also was pure DNA. Viruses are tiny particles, far smaller than bacteria, that exist on the border between living and nonliving things. They cannot reproduce directly, but they can attach themselves to cells and inject their genes, which then force the cells to create new viruses. The fact that the substance they used to do this was a nucleic acid suggested that nucleic acid, not protein, was the carrier of genetic information.

But how could DNA carry information? A few scientists suspected that the answer to this question lay in the structure of the

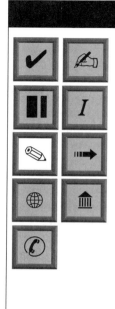

SOLVING PROBLEMS

X-RAY CRYSTALLOGRAPHY

In X-ray crystallography, a beam of X rays is passed through a solid. This solid must be in the form of an orderly structure called a crystal. The rays bounce off some of the atoms in the molecules within the crystal. This affects the angles at which the rays strike a photographic plate on the other side of the crystal. The resulting photograph shows a pattern of dark dots or smears on a light background. Interpreted by experts, such photographs reveal important facts about the structure of the molecules. British scientist Lawrence Bragg invented the X-ray crystallography technique in 1912. In 1934 two other British scientists, Desmond Bernal and W. T. Astbury, showed that it could be used to reveal the structure of large, complex molecules such as proteins and nucleic acids.

DNA molecule. DNA molecules are as large as those of proteins, and, like proteins, they are made of combinations of smaller molecules. They have a "backbone" made up of identical units, each of which consists of one molecule of a sugar called deoxyribose and one molecule of phosphate (a phosphorus-containing compound). Attached to each backbone unit is another kind of small molecule called a base. In DNA there are four types of bases: adenine, guanine, cytosine, and thymine.

Scientists knew about the backbone and the bases, but they did not know how these smaller molecules were arranged within the DNA molecule. They had only two clues about the arrangement. First, a technique called X-ray crystallography suggested that the DNA backbone might have the shape of a coil, or helix, a shape that had also been found in protein molecules. Second, in the late 1940s, Austrian-born chemist Erwin Chargaff showed a relationship among the quantities of bases in any DNA molecule: there was always just as much cytosine as guanine and just as much adenine as thymine.

A Race, a Siege, a Conquest

Science historian Horace Freeland Judson has written, "The elucidation [working out] of the structure of deoxyribonucleic acid . . . [was] a concentration of forces, a siege, a conquest." At the start of the 1950s, when many biologists still doubted the importance of DNA, only three groups of researchers were far-sighted enough to attempt that conquest. One was in the United States, and the other two were in Britain.

The American group, at Caltech, was headed by a chemist named Linus Pauling. One of the British groups was at King's College in London. Its leader was Maurice Wilkins, who had come from New Zealand. Working with him was British chemist Rosalind Franklin, an expert in X-ray crystallography. The third group laying siege to DNA worked at Cambridge, one of Britain's two most famous universities. One of the scientists in this group

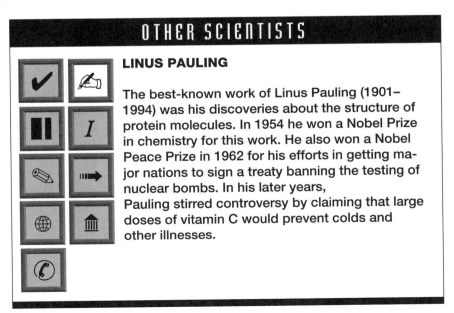

OTHER SCIENTISTS

LINUS PAULING

The best-known work of Linus Pauling (1901–1994) was his discoveries about the structure of protein molecules. In 1954 he won a Nobel Prize in chemistry for this work. He also won a Nobel Peace Prize in 1962 for his efforts in getting major nations to sign a treaty banning the testing of nuclear bombs. In his later years, Pauling stirred controversy by claiming that large doses of vitamin C would prevent colds and other illnesses.

was British, the other American. It was this group that finally won the race to understand DNA.

The American at Cambridge, James Dewey Watson, was the younger of the pair. Born in Chicago in 1928, he entered the University of Chicago when he was only 15 years old. At first he planned to study birds, but while doing graduate work at Indiana University he became interested in genetics. He received his Ph.D. from the university in 1950.

While doing further study in Europe, Watson met Maurice Wilkins in 1951. From Wilkins he learned that DNA, in which Watson was already interested, could form crystals and therefore could be studied by X-ray crystallography. This meant that DNA must have regular, or repeated, features in its structure. Watson became convinced that the shape of a DNA molecule would be "simple as well as pretty."

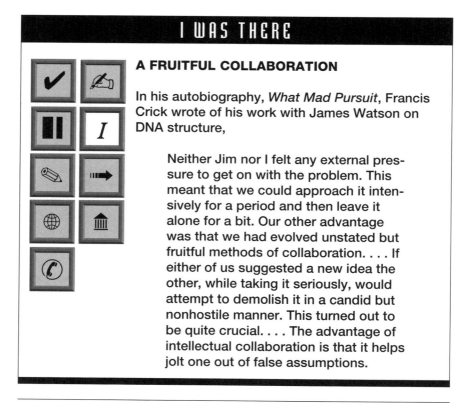

I WAS THERE

A FRUITFUL COLLABORATION

In his autobiography, *What Mad Pursuit*, Francis Crick wrote of his work with James Watson on DNA structure,

> Neither Jim nor I felt any external pressure to get on with the problem. This meant that we could approach it intensively for a period and then leave it alone for a bit. Our other advantage was that we had evolved unstated but fruitful methods of collaboration. . . . If either of us suggested a new idea the other, while taking it seriously, would attempt to demolish it in a candid but nonhostile manner. This turned out to be quite crucial. . . . The advantage of intellectual collaboration is that it helps jolt one out of false assumptions.

CONNECTIONS

COMPUTER MODEL BUILDING

Today, chemists and molecular biologists can build models of molecules without using for a machine shop. They do their model building on computers. Computer model-building programs show different kinds of atoms or molecules in different colors. They can turn the models so that scientists can view them from any angle. Scientists can type in different specifications and see instantly what effects these changes have on their model. Scientists use computer model building to design new drugs, plastics, and other useful substances.

Watson joined the Cavendish Laboratory at Cambridge, where scientists were using X-ray crystallography to study protein molecules. There he met 35-year-old British scientist Francis Harry Compton Crick. At the time he met Watson, Crick still did not have his Ph.D. degree. He had received a B.S. in physics, but his scientific career had been interrupted by World War II.

"I . . . immediately discovered the fun of talking to Francis," Watson later wrote. Crick, for his part, has said,

> Jim and I hit it off immediately, partly because our interests were astonishingly similar and partly, I suspect, because a certain youthful arrogance, a ruthlessness, and an impatience with sloppy thinking came naturally to both of us.

The most important interest the two men shared was in DNA, which Watson called the "most golden of all molecules." Both were convinced that the structure of DNA contained the secret of heredity. They were sure that discovering DNA's structure would make them famous—if they could solve the puzzle before the King's College or the Caltech team did.

Watson and Crick attempted to work out the structure of DNA mostly by thinking and talking. They also used a technique called model building, which had helped Linus Pauling learn about protein molecules. Their models, whose metal parts were made to order by the Cambridge machine shop, drew on details of spacing and angles of atoms that others had learned through X-ray crystallography and other techniques. The models let the men see and manipulate possible structures for the DNA molecule in three dimensions.

Moment of Discovery

"In the process of [scientific] discovery," Horace Freeland Judson says, "there comes a unique moment: where great confusion reigned, the shape of an answer springs out—or at least the form of a question." For James Watson, such a moment came on

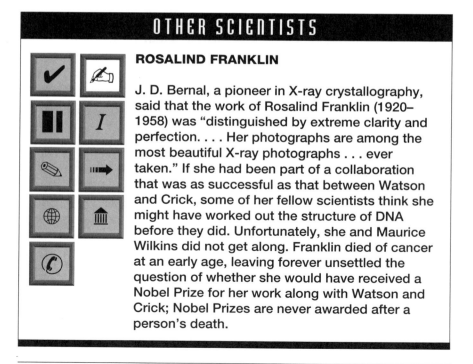

OTHER SCIENTISTS

ROSALIND FRANKLIN

J. D. Bernal, a pioneer in X-ray crystallography, said that the work of Rosalind Franklin (1920–1958) was "distinguished by extreme clarity and perfection. . . . Her photographs are among the most beautiful X-ray photographs . . . ever taken." If she had been part of a collaboration that was as successful as that between Watson and Crick, some of her fellow scientists think she might have worked out the structure of DNA before they did. Unfortunately, she and Maurice Wilkins did not get along. Franklin died of cancer at an early age, leaving forever unsettled the question of whether she would have received a Nobel Prize for her work along with Watson and Crick; Nobel Prizes are never awarded after a person's death.

January 30, 1953, when he visited Maurice Wilkins at King's College. In spite of being rivals in the DNA race, the two had become friends. On this visit Wilkins showed Watson an X-ray photograph that Rosalind Franklin had recently made of a DNA crystal. He did not ask Franklin's permission to do so.

This photograph was much clearer than any other that had ever been made. As he looked at it, Watson reported later, "my mouth fell open and my pulse began to race." He realized that the DNA molecule's backbone most likely consisted of two helices (plural of *helix*), wound around each other. The bases had to be inside the molecule, between the two backbones.

Watson hurried back to tell Crick of his discovery. Over the next month, the two tried to figure out how the bases might be arranged within the DNA molecule. At first Watson thought the bases might appear as pairs of the same kind of molecule—adenine and adenine, for example. That did not fit what was known about the space between the backbones, however. Two of the bases, adenine and guanine, were larger than the other two. Pairs of large bases were too big to fit between the twined backbones, while pairs of the smaller bases were too little.

Too impatient to wait for new metal models to be built, Watson cut model pieces from cardboard. As he played with the cardboard bases, he saw that a pair consisting of adenine, a large base, and thymine, a small one, had exactly the same size and shape as a pair made up of guanine and cytosine. Bonds between the bases' hydrogen atoms could hold such pairs together. A pairing of adenine with thymine and guanine with cytosine would also fit with Erwin Chargaff's finding about the proportions of bases in the DNA molecule. The base pairs fit nicely if placed horizontally between the two vertical backbones, like steps on a twisted ladder.

As soon as Crick came into their shared office on the morning of February 28, Watson showed him the matching cardboard base pairs. Crick made the further observation that such pairing would mean that the sequence of bases along one DNA backbone had to be the exact reverse of the sequence along the other.

Excitedly Watson and Crick wrote up a short scientific paper that described their proposed structure. They persuaded Watson's

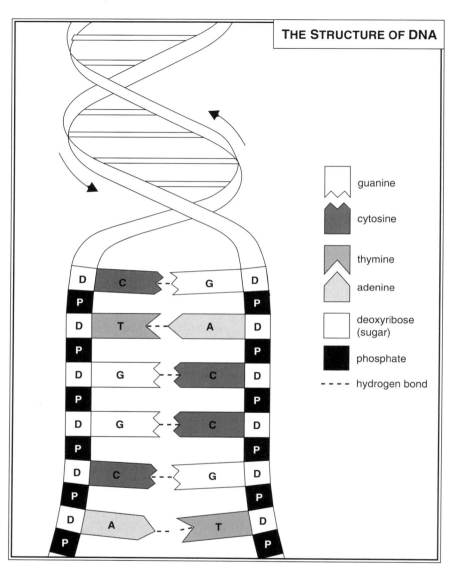

THE STRUCTURE OF DNA

guanine

cytosine

thymine

adenine

deoxyribose (sugar)

phosphate

- - - - hydrogen bond

James Watson and Francis Crick discovered the structure of deoxyribonucleic acid (DNA), the chemical that carries inherited information, in 1953. Each DNA molecule is made up of two "backbones" composed of alternating smaller molecules of phosphate (P) and deoxyribose (D), a sugar. The backbones both have the shape of a helix, or coil, and they twine around each other. Inside the backbones, like rungs on a ladder, are four kinds of molecules called bases. The bases always exist in pairs, connected by hydrogen bonds. Adenine (A) always pairs with thymine (T), and cytosine (C) always pairs with guanine (G).

visiting sister, Elizabeth, to type the paper. "We told her that she was participating in perhaps the most famous event in biology since Darwin's book," Watson said later. The paper appeared in the prestigious British science journal *Nature* on April 25, 1953.

Only one understated sentence near the end of Watson and Crick's paper hinted at the importance of their discovery: "It has not escaped our notice that the specific pairing we have postulated immediately suggests a possible copying mechanism for the genetic material." With less restraint, Crick wrote to his son, "We think we have found the basic mechanism by which life comes from life."

I WAS THERE

THE SECRET OF LIFE

In *The Double Helix*, his memoir about the discovery of DNA's structure, James Watson recalls the day he and Francis Crick realized that they had found the right structure at last.

> Upon his arrival [at their shared office] Francis did not get more than halfway through the door before I let loose that the answer to everything was in our hands. . . . We both knew that we would not be home [sure their structure was right] until a complete model was built in which all the [features fitted with the X-ray data]. . . . The implications . . . were too important to risk crying wolf. Thus I felt slightly queasy when at lunch Francis winged into the Eagle [a nearby bar] to tell everyone . . . that we had found the secret of life.

How DNA Reproduces

About five weeks after their first paper, Watson and Crick published a second one that explained the cryptic sentence in the first. If DNA carried hereditary information, they said, it had to be able to duplicate itself, because the chromosomes duplicated during cell division. They believed that the key to DNA's reproduction lay in its mirror-image structure. Just before a cell divided, the weak hydrogen bonds between the pairs of bases in its DNA molecules broke. That made the molecules split lengthwise, like a zipper unzipping. Each base then attracted its "mate," complete with an attached backbone segment, from among the free-floating materials in the cell nucleus. An adenine molecule always attracted a thymine and vice versa, and the same for cytosine and guanine. The result was two identical DNA strands where there had been one.

Watson and Crick's DNA discovery won them a Nobel Prize in 1962. It also gave an enormous boost to a new scientific discipline called molecular biology. This discipline focused on the structure and activities of molecules in living things and on the ways those molecules contributed to life. The name *molecular biology* had first been used in 1938 by Warren Weaver of the Rockefeller Foundation, who called the new field "a . . . branch of science . . . which may prove as revolutionary . . . as the discovery of the living cell." Watson and Crick were leading supporters of the molecular approach. Crick, for instance, once stated that the ultimate aim of modern biology was to explain "*all* biology in terms of physics and chemistry."

The Genetic Code

After his and Watson's breakthrough discovery, Francis Crick continued to do research on DNA. He wanted to learn how a DNA molecule carried information and how it translated that

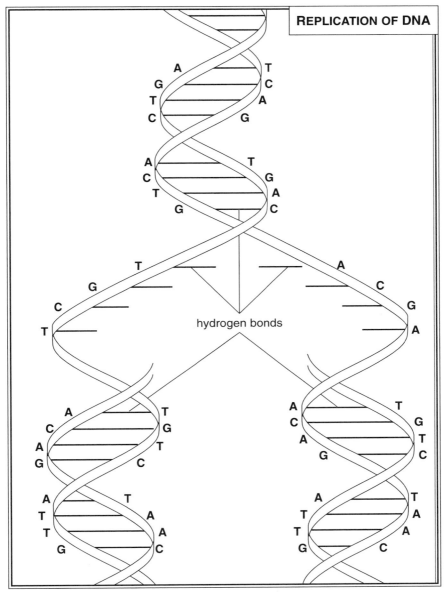

REPLICATION OF DNA

hydrogen bonds

DNA's structure explains its power to duplicate itself. When a cell gets ready to divide, the hydrogen bonds between the bases dissolve and the DNA molecule splits along its length like a zipper unzipping. Each half then attracts bases and backbones from among molecules in the cell, forming the same pairs of bases that had existed before. The result is two identical DNA molecules where there had been one.

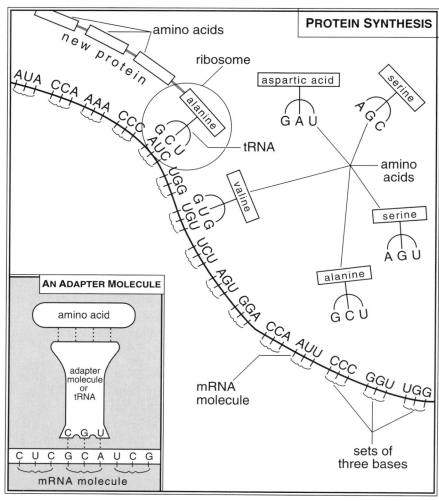

As a first step in making a protein, part of a DNA molecule (a gene) uses itself as a pattern to form a matching stretch of messenger RNA (m RNA). RNA is like DNA except that the sugar ribose instead of deoxyribose appears in its backbone and a base called uracil (U) substitutes for thymine. In the messenger RNA, as in the DNA, each group of three bases is a "code word" representing one of the amino acids that can be combined to make a protein. When the messenger RNA moves into the cytoplasm of the cell, it attracts matching short stretches of transfer RNA (tRNA). Each molecule of transfer RNA acts like a tugboat, towing a single amino acid molecule. With the help of an organelle called a ribosome, the transfer RNA molecules lock onto the matching parts of the messenger RNA. The amino acids they carry are then joined, forming a protein.

information into proteins. In 1957 he proposed that the order, or sequence, of bases in a DNA molecule was a code that stood for the sequence of amino acids in protein molecules. If each amino acid was represented by a set of three bases, he pointed out, there would be 64 possible combinations, more than enough to represent all 20 amino acids. "Such an arrangement can carry an enormous amount of information," Crick said.

Marshall Nirenberg of the National Institutes of Health and other molecular biologists set out to "crack" the DNA code, determining by experiment which amino acid each combination of three bases stood for. Each amino acid proved to be represented by several such groups, and some additional groups marked the beginning or end of a gene. (Each DNA molecule contains hundreds or even thousands of genes.) By the mid-1960s, researchers had a "dictionary" that included all 64 three-base combinations. The code seemed to have the same meaning in virtually all living things.

Once the DNA code was known, scientists began working out the base sequence of particular genes. If they knew the sequence of a gene, they could learn what protein it made. They could also find it on a chromosome by making an artificial stretch of DNA with the same sequence, using chemicals that contained radioactive atoms. The artificial gene would stick to the real gene, marking its location. The pair of genes could be identified by tests that detected radioactivity.

Scientists also learned that DNA molecules contain more than just instructions for making proteins. For instance, some genes tell others when to turn on (begin producing protein) or off (stop producing protein) or how much protein to produce. This helps to explain the fact that so puzzled Thomas Hunt Morgan: how cells in the body of a living thing can be so different, even though they all contain the same genes. Only 10 to 20 percent of the genes in a given cell are ever active, and many of these are active only at a certain stage in the cell's life.

Even before the details of the DNA code were worked out, Francis Crick and others set out to learn the mechanism that allows DNA to produce proteins. First, they found, DNA makes a copy of itself in the form of RNA (ribonucleic acid), which is like DNA except that it has a different kind of sugar (ribose) in its backbone and in place of thymine it has a different base, uracil. DNA normally cannot leave the cell nucleus, but this so-called messenger RNA can travel from the nucleus into the cytoplasm, the jellylike material that makes up the cell body.

In the cytoplasm, RNA encounters small bodies called ribosomes. A ribosome rolls along the messenger RNA molecule, at the same time attracting from the cytoplasm the amino acids represented by each three-base "letter" of the translated RNA code. The amino acids are towed by what Crick called "adaptor" molecules, which were later found to be another form of RNA called transfer RNA. Finally these amino acids join together, forming the protein. They are then released from the RNA and the ribosome to carry out their work in the cell.

On the basis of this mechanism, Crick proposed what became known as the "Central Dogma" (strongly held belief) of modern genetics: "Once 'information' has passed into protein, *it cannot get out again.*" In other words, changes in genes produce changes in

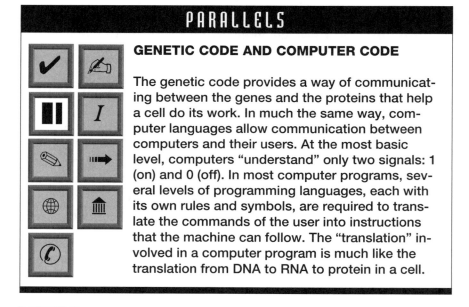

PARALLELS

GENETIC CODE AND COMPUTER CODE

The genetic code provides a way of communicating between the genes and the proteins that help a cell do its work. In much the same way, computer languages allow communication between computers and their users. At the most basic level, computers "understand" only two signals: 1 (on) and 0 (off). In most computer programs, several levels of programming languages, each with its own rules and symbols, are required to translate the commands of the user into instructions that the machine can follow. The "translation" involved in a computer program is much like the translation from DNA to RNA to protein in a cell.

proteins, but changed proteins cannot change genes. Scientists later discovered, however, that the Central Dogma does not always hold true.

The Human Genome Project

While Francis Crick continued his career as a researcher, James Watson returned to the United States and became a teacher and administrator. In 1968, he became director of Cold Spring Harbor Laboratory on Long Island, New York. Watson modernized this famous laboratory and focused its research on the biology of cancer, which has proved to be intimately related to genetics.

In 1989, when Watson was 60 years old, the U.S. government chose him to head the newest and biggest genetic project of all: the Human Genome Project, sometimes called "biology's moon shot." The goal of this project, which is expected to cost $3 billion, is to work out the base sequence of every gene—50,000 to 100,000 of them, totaling about 3 billion base pairs—in the genome, or complete genetic makeup, of human beings. The project, which involves scientists in research centers around the world, is currently scheduled to be completed in 2005.

The "genome" sequenced by the project is a composite one, based on the individual genomes of men and women from a variety of races and ethnic groups. This composite approach works because, although different people have different forms of particular genes (one might have an eye color gene that codes for blue eyes and one an eye color gene that codes for brown eyes, for instance), for the most part they have the same genes in the same order on their chromosomes.

The Human Genome Project is expected to have major impacts on the diagnosis and possible prevention or treatment, not only of inherited diseases but of more common illnesses such as cancer and heart disease, which often have a genetic component. (The disease itself is not inherited, but a tendency to get it is.) "I think that many major diseases will be understood when we can get their genetic basis," Watson has said. He remains a strong supporter of the genome project, but he resigned as head of the project in 1992 because of disagreements with the director of the National Institutes of Health, which cosponsors the project.

Horace Freeland Judson has said that "biology has proceeded by 'openings up'" rather than through the complete changes of ideas that have often occurred in physics. James Watson and Francis Crick's discovery of the structure of DNA surely sparked one of the biggest "openings up" of all. Scientist and science historian Peter Medawar has said that the unraveling of the structure of DNA and the discoveries about how genes work that followed it are "the greatest achievement of science in the 20th century."

Chronology of the Structure and Function of DNA

1869	Johann Miescher discovers nucleic acids
1916	Francis Crick born in Northampton, England
1928	James Watson born in Chicago, Illinois
1938	Scientific field of molecular biology defined
1944	Oswald Avery shows that bacteria's inheritance can be changed through use of pure DNA
late 1940s	Erwin Chargaff shows relationship among bases in DNA
1951	Watson and Crick meet in Cambridge, England
1953	Watson and Crick discover structure of DNA
1957	Crick proposes idea of DNA base sequence as code containing instructions for making protein
1961–65	Genetic code deciphered Process by which DNA makes protein worked out
1962	Watson, Crick, and Maurice Wilkins win Nobel Prize for discovery of structure of DNA
1989	Watson named head of Human Genome Project
1992	Resigns position of Human Genome Project

Further Reading

Crick, Francis. *What Mad Pursuit*. New York: Basic Books, 1988. Crick's autobiography; less entertaining than Watson's book but perhaps more balanced. Somewhat difficult reading.

"Crick, Francis (Harry Compton)." *Current Biography Yearbook* 1983. New York: H. W. Wilson, 1983. Good biographical article about Crick, with quotes from interviews.

Jaroff, Leon. "The Gene Hunt." *Time*, March 20, 1989. Article about the Human Genome Project, written near its beginning.

————. "Happy Birthday, Double Helix." *Time*, March 15, 1993. Popular article on the 50th anniversary of Watson and Crick's discovery reviews some of the discoveries in genetics and genetic engineering since that time.

Judson, Horace Freeland. *The Eighth Day of Creation*. New York: Simon and Schuster, 1979. Describes Watson and Crick's discovery of DNA structure and other key discoveries in genetics and molecular biology from the mid-1930s to about 1970. Difficult but interesting reading.

Sayre, Anne. *Rosalind Franklin and DNA*. New York: Norton, 1975. Gives another view of the race to find the structure of DNA.

Sherrow, Victoria. *Great Scientists*. New York: Facts On File, 1992. Includes a good chapter on Watson.

Watson, James D. *The Double Helix*. New York: New American Library, 1968. Lively but biased memoir about the discovery of the structure of DNA.

"Watson, James (Dewey)." *Current Biography Yearbook* 1990. New York: H. W. Wilson, 1990. Good biographical article about Watson, with quotes from interviews.

NOTES

p. 41   "The elucidation . . ." Quoted in N. A. Tiley. *Discovering DNA* (New York: Van Nostrand Reinhold, 1983), p. 53.

p. 42   "simple as well as pretty." Quoted in "Watson, James (Dewey)." *Current Biography Yearbook 1990* (New York: H. W. Wilson, 1990), p. 607.

p. 42   "Neither Jim nor I . . ." Crick, p. 70.

p. 43   "I . . . immediately discovered . . ." Quoted in "Watson, James (Dewey)," p. 607.

p. 43   "Jim and I hit it off . . ." Francis Crick. *What Mad Pursuit* (New York: Basic Books, 1988), p. 64.

p. 43   "most golden . . ." Quoted in "Watson, James (Dewey)," p. 606.

p. 44   In the process . . ." Quoted in Tiley, p. 53.

p. 44   "distinguished by extreme . . ." Quoted in Lisa Yount. *Twentieth-Century Women Scientists* (New York: Facts On File, 1996), p. 71.

p. 45   "my mouth fell open . . ." James D. Watson. *The Double Helix* (New York: New American Library, 1968), pp. 107–8.

p. 47   "We told her . . ." Quoted in Victoria Sherrow. *Great Scientists* (New York: Facts On File, 1992), p. 135.

p. 47   "It has not escaped . . ." Quoted in Dennis L. Breo. "The Double Helix—Watson and Crick's 'Freak Find' of How Like Begets Like," *Journal of the American Medical Association*, February 24, 1993, p. 1040.

p. 47   "We think we have found . . ." Quoted in Walter Bodmer and Robin McKie. *The Book of Man* (New York: Scribner, 1994), p. 43.

p. 47   "Upon his arrival . . ." Watson, pp. 125–26.

p. 48   "a . . . branch of science . . ." Quoted in R. C. Olby, et al., eds. *Companion to the History of Modern Science* (London: Routledge, 1990), p. 504.

p. 48   "*all* biology . . ." Quoted in Olby, p. 509.

p. 51   "Such an arrangement . . ." Quoted in Sherrow, p. 135.

p. 52   "Once 'information' has passed . . ." Quoted in "Crick, Francis (Harry Compton)." *Current Biography Yearbook 1983* (New York: H. W. Wilson, 1983), p. 70.

pp. 52–53   "I think that many . . ." Quoted in "Watson, James (Dewey),"
p. 609.

p. 54   "biology has proceeded . . ." Quoted in Olby, p. 516.

p. 54   "the greatest achievement . . ." Quoted in Breo, p. 1040.

4

The Gene Deli

STANLEY COHEN, HERBERT BOYER, AND GENETIC ENGINEERING

During a conversation in a delicatessen, Stanford University molecular biologist Stanley Cohen, shown here, and Herbert Boyer of the University of California at San Francisco invented genetic engineering. (Courtesy Stanford University News Service)

. . . .

It seems fitting that genetic engineering got its start in a delicatessen. Like the server behind the counter in a deli, genetic engineers can slice genes to order, sandwich them in with genes from other living things, and wrap up the package "to go." In doing so, they have created completely new kinds of organisms and opened up possibilities that will greatly affect science, human society, and even, perhaps, all life on this planet.

A Chat over Corned Beef

It wasn't the server in that Hawaiian delicatessen who had the inspiration in November 1972, though. It was two molecular biologists, Stanley Cohen of Stanford University and Herbert Boyer of the University of California at San Francisco (UCSF). They had dropped in for a late night snack after a long day of meetings at a conference in Honolulu.

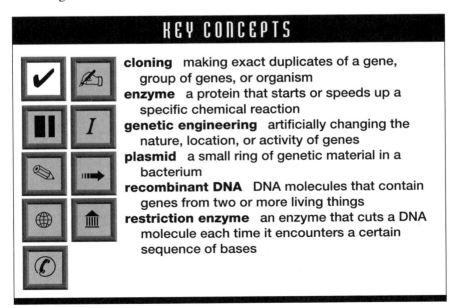

KEY CONCEPTS

cloning   making exact duplicates of a gene, group of genes, or organism

enzyme   a protein that starts or speeds up a specific chemical reaction

genetic engineering   artificially changing the nature, location, or activity of genes

plasmid   a small ring of genetic material in a bacterium

recombinant DNA   DNA molecules that contain genes from two or more living things

restriction enzyme   an enzyme that cuts a DNA molecule each time it encounters a certain sequence of bases

Cohen had heard a speech that Boyer gave that day, and he was eager to learn more about the work Boyer was doing. When Cohen began to talk about his own research, Boyer became equally interested. As they devoured their corned beef sandwiches, the two men came to realize that their projects were like two halves of a puzzle: each had tools and techniques that the other badly needed. By joining forces, they might be able to do something truly remarkable.

Boyer, a husky former high school football star born in Derry, Pennsylvania, in 1936, was working on a group of chemicals found in certain bacteria. Called restriction enzymes, these substances slice through strands of DNA wherever they find a particular sequence of bases. The bacteria use their "molecular scissors" to snip invading viruses in two before the viruses have a chance to reproduce and kill the bacteria. To scientists like Boyer, the enzymes offered a way of dividing immensely long DNA molecules into manageable—and predictable—chunks. Different restriction enzymes cut DNA at different sequences, so molecular biologists could choose how they would slice their DNA by deciding which enzyme to use. About a hundred different restriction enzymes were eventually discovered.

One of the most useful things about restriction enzymes, Boyer told Cohen, was that these "scissors" were not very sharp. Instead of cutting cleanly through a DNA molecule, they left an incomplete sequence of bases dangling from each end of the cut piece. For instance, Boyer was working with an enzyme that was called EcoR1 because it was the first restriction enzyme discovered in *Escherichia coli (E. coli)*, a common and usually harmless bacterium that grows in the human intestine. This enzyme always left a single-stranded sequence of the bases T-T-A-A (thymine, thymine, adenine, adenine) at one end and a mirror-image strand, A-A-T-T, at the other.

Just as happened when DNA reproduced, these dangling bases were strongly attracted to other bases that would complete their usual pairings. That meant that the sequence from one snipped piece of DNA would attach easily to the opposite end of another piece of DNA that had been cut by the same enzyme. It didn't matter what type of living thing the other piece came from. Other chemicals called ligases could then be used to glue the "sticky ends" together.

Cohen told Boyer that he was doing something different with bacteria. In 1965, scientists who studied microbes had discovered that, in addition to the large, ring-shaped DNA molecule that carries most of their genetic information, bacteria often contain smaller rings of DNA called plasmids. Each plasmid holds only a few genes. Bacteria do not exchange genes through sex as many living things do, but they sometimes exchange plasmids during a process called conjugation. Cohen had found ways to imitate this process, removing plasmids from bacterial cells and inserting them into other bacteria.

The First Gene Splicing

By the time they finished their sandwiches, Boyer and Cohen had planned a series of experiments that would combine their knowledge. In the spring of 1973, after they returned to California, they began carrying out those experiments. With the help of coworkers Annie Chang and Robert Helling, the two first used Boyer's EcoR1 enzyme to cut open some of Cohen's plasmids. Because of the "sticky ends" left by the inefficient molecular scissors, they could join two different plasmids together to make a single large one. Cohen called the new plasmid a chimera, after a monster from ancient Greek legend that was part lion, part goat, and part snake.

The plasmids used in the pair's first experiment came from two different strains of *E. coli*, which had become a "workhorse" bacterial species, as common in molecular biology and genetics labs as Thomas Morgan's fruit flies had once been. One plasmid carried a gene that made the bacteria resistant to the antibiotic tetracycline, while the other had a gene that produced resistance to kanamycin, a different antibiotic. Boyer and Cohen put the altered plasmids into bacteria that normally would be killed by

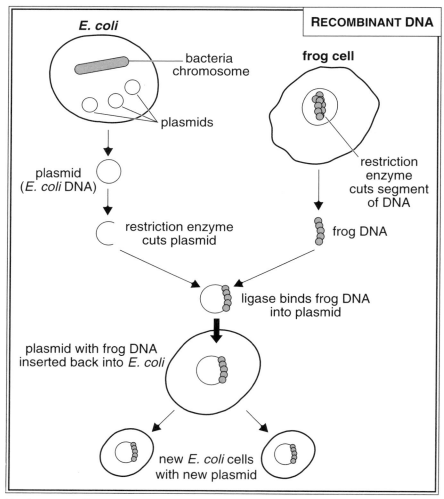

RECOMBINANT DNA

E. coli

bacteria chromosome

plasmids

frog cell

plasmid (*E. coli* DNA)

restriction enzyme cuts segment of DNA

restriction enzyme cuts plasmid

frog DNA

ligase binds frog DNA into plasmid

plasmid with frog DNA inserted back into *E. coli*

new *E. coli* cells with new plasmid

In their groundbreaking gene-splicing experiments, Stanley Cohen and Herbert Boyer first broke up cells of a common bacterium, E. coli, *and took out some of the small, ring-shaped pieces of DNA called plasmids. They then used a restriction enzyme to cut the plasmids open. They used the same enzyme to extract genes from other living things, such as viruses or frogs. The enzyme left the same kind of "sticky ends" on both the plasmids and the genes, allowing them to join easily. A second cell chemical called a ligase bound the genes in place and closed each plasmid. The researchers then inserted the plasmids carrying the foreign genes into other* E. coli *bacteria and showed that the foreign genes could make their normal proteins. When the bacteria multiplied, the added genes were duplicated along with the bacteria's own genetic material.*

both types of drug. They then transferred the bacteria to a culture dish that contained the two antibiotics. Some of the bacteria survived, which meant that both resistance genes were making their proteins in their new home. For the first time, human beings had moved genes from one kind of living thing to another and showed that the genes could function afterward.

The first experiment did not go too far beyond nature, since bacteria often exchanged plasmids on their own. In a second experiment, however, Boyer and Cohen combined plasmids from two different kinds of bacteria. A third experiment went still further, putting a gene from a frog into a plasmid. In both cases, the new plasmids functioned when put into bacteria, and they were reproduced when the bacteria multiplied. The bacteria containing these plasmids were essentially new kinds of organisms.

Cohen called his and Boyer's new technique "recombinant DNA." It later also became known as gene splicing. Other molecular biologists were quick to realize its potential. After hearing Boyer describe the work in conversation at a scientific meeting in June 1973, one scientist summed up everyone's reaction by saying, "Well, now we can put together any DNA we want to." In the next few years, scientists not only moved genes from one living thing to another but cloned or duplicated genes, altered them by changing their sequence of bases, and changed their activity by moving them to different places on the genome. All these artificial changes became known as genetic engineering.

But Is It Safe?

Two floors above Cohen's laboratory at Stanford was the laboratory of another molecular biologist named Paul Berg. Berg probably would have created genetically engineered organisms before Cohen and Boyer—if concern about the possible results of his experiments had not stopped him.

A few months before Boyer and Cohen's experiments began, Berg removed a gene from SV40, a type of virus that infected monkeys. He inserted it into the small, circular genome of another virus called lambda, which attacked bacteria. Lacking Boyer's restriction enzymes, he laboriously attached sticky ends to his virus genes by chemical means. He then joined them with a ligase. He thus became the first person to combine genes from two different types of living things. He did not put the genes into an organism or show that they functioned, however.

Berg had planned to use lambda as a vector, or carrier, to insert SV40 genes into *E. coli.* When Robert Pollack, a geneticist working at Cold Spring Harbor, heard about this proposed experiment, however, he phoned Berg in alarm. SV40 was harmless in monkeys, he pointed out, but it could cause cancer in mice and hamsters. Pollack was worried about the possible danger of inserting potential cancer-causing genes into a bacterium that could live in human intestines.

Berg decided that it would be wise to heed Pollack's warning, and he called off his experiments. When he heard about the work being done by Boyer, Cohen, and others, he became concerned about the safety of some of their experiments as well.

Late in 1973, Berg and 77 other molecular biologists sent a letter to the prestigious American scientific journal *Science.* It recommended that the National Institutes of Health (NIH), the chief medical research organizations sponsored by the U.S. government, establish safety guidelines for recombinant DNA experiments.

The scientists' call for caution went still further in a second letter, published in July 1974. Berg and the other signers of the letter asked other scientists to agree to a moratorium, or temporary halt, on some kinds of gene-altering research until the possible hazards of such work had been evaluated and more adequate safety precautions had been developed. The scientists feared that dangerous traits, such as the ability to cause cancer or resist antibiotics, would become incorporated into bacteria that might accidentally escape from genetics laboratories and go on to infect humans.

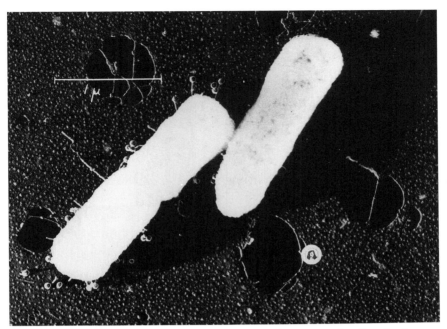

These white bacteria are Escherichia coli, *a type of bacterium that lives in the human intestine. They were used in many of the first experiments in genetic engineering. The dark particles next to them are a type of virus called lambda, which invades these bacteria. The viruses can be used to carry foreign genes into the bacteria.* (Courtesy American Society for Microbiology Archives Collection)

These safety fears resulted in a groundbreaking meeting of 140 molecular biologists at Asilomar, California, in February 1975. The group concluded,

> Most of the work on . . . recombinant DNA molecules should proceed, provided that appropriate safeguards, principally biological and physical barriers adequate to contain the newly created organisms, are employed.

The scientists divided recombinant DNA experiments into four categories according to the degree of danger the experiments presented. They then worked out guidelines for conducting each category of experiment safely. In the most dangerous experiments, for instance, lab workers might be required to wear protective garments much like space suits or to handle bacterial cultures only with gloves that reached through openings in the walls of a sealed room. The Asilomar group also recommended that bacteria used in genetic engineering experiments be weakened so they could not live outside the laboratory.

In 1976, the NIH drew up guidelines for genetic engineering experiments that were very similar to the ones written at the Asilomar meeting. All scientists receiving funding from the federal government had to follow the guidelines. Most other American researchers, especially those at universities, also agreed to do so. In addition, the NIH established a Recombinant DNA Advisory Committee (RAC) to approve new genetic engineering experiments.

Fears of genetic engineering died down somewhat over the next several years as experiments proceeded without creating any Frankenstein monsters. Most of the NIH guidelines were dropped in 1980. The RAC, however, remained in existence.

ISSUES

FEARS OF A NEW TECHNOLOGY

The public, the media, and some nonscientific groups expressed strong fears of genetic engineering in the late 1970s and early 1980s. In 1980, for example, the general secretaries of the National Council of Churches, the United States Catholic Conference, and the Synagogue Council of America issued a joint statement warning of "a new era of fundamental danger triggered by the rapid growth of genetic engineering." An economist and writer named Jeremy Rifkin protested against the new technology in a 1983 book called *Algeny*, which became quite popular.

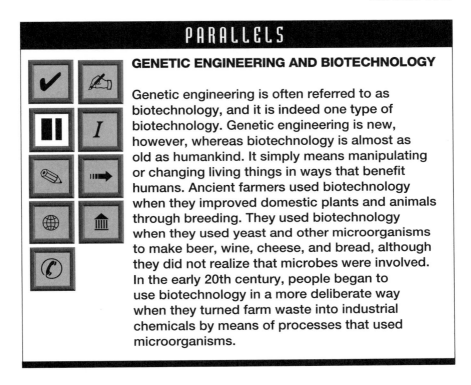

PARALLELS

GENETIC ENGINEERING AND BIOTECHNOLOGY

Genetic engineering is often referred to as biotechnology, and it is indeed one type of biotechnology. Genetic engineering is new, however, whereas biotechnology is almost as old as humankind. It simply means manipulating or changing living things in ways that benefit humans. Ancient farmers used biotechnology when they improved domestic plants and animals through breeding. They used biotechnology when they used yeast and other microorganisms to make beer, wine, cheese, and bread, although they did not realize that microbes were involved. In the early 20th century, people began to use biotechnology in a more deliberate way when they turned farm waste into industrial chemicals by means of processes that used microorganisms.

Bacterial Bonanzas

Even while scientific and public fear of gene-splicing was at its height, excitement about the new technology's promise was equally strong. Many people hoped it would produce new ways to treat disease or increase the world's food supply. In addition, farsighted businesspeople began to suspect that genetic engineering might be a way to make a great deal of money.

One of the first scientists to grasp this idea was Herbert Boyer. He and Stanley Cohen had given all patent rights to their original discovery to their respective universities. In 1976, however, a young venture capitalist named Robert Swanson persuaded Boyer to join him in starting a business that would use genetic engineering techniques. They called their company Genentech, for GEnetic ENgineering TECHnology. In October 1980, at which time the company had produced no salable product at all, inves-

SOCIAL IMPACT

PATENTING LIVING THINGS

When genetic engineering began, the U.S. Patent Office held that living things could not be patented. A Supreme Court decision in 1980, however, changed this ruling. The first patent for a genetically engineered organism went to Ananda M. Chakrabarty, an Indian-born scientist then working for General Electric, for a new type of bacterium that ate oil and could be used to clean up oil spills. Engineered genes can now be patented as well. Biotechnology companies applauded these decisions, but others have questioned whether patenting living things or their genes is ethical.

tors' optimism about Genentech's future was so great that when its stock was first offered to the public, the price rose from $35 to $89 per share in a few minutes. One newspaper called Genentech stock "the most spectacular new stock offering in at least a decade."

Genentech, like similar companies formed soon afterward by other scientists and entrepreneurs, drew on a basic quality of bacteria: they multiply at a speed that makes Morgan's fruit flies seem as slow as Mendel's peas must have seemed to Morgan. Bacteria double their number every 20 minutes, so one bacterium can produce millions more like itself in a single day. If a foreign gene has been inserted into the bacterium, that gene is duplicated along with the rest of the bacterium's genome. The result is millions of identical copies, or clones, of the gene, each able to produce its characteristic protein. Bacteria thus become tiny factories, potentially able to churn out useful proteins in tremendous amounts.

The first commercial product that Genentech made in its bacterial factories was insulin, a hormone that controls the breakdown of sugar in the body. Insulin is normally made by special cells in the pancreas, an organ in the abdomen that helps with digestion. If those cells become damaged so that they can no longer make insulin, the result is diabetes. Serious forms of this illness can be fatal unless its victims take insulin, usually in the form of daily injections.

Insulin can be extracted in relatively large amounts from the pancreases of cattle and pigs, so diabetics could obtain this vital drug fairly cheaply even before genetic engineering. Pig and cow insulin, however, are not exactly the same as human insulin, and about 5 percent of people with diabetes are allergic to these animal substances. Bacteria containing the gene that produces human insulin make a substance essentially identical to the human form of the hormone. Even though the percentage of diabetics who were allergic was small, 5 percent of 1.8 million diabetics in the United States alone amounted to enough potential customers that Boyer and Swanson believed they could make a profit. Besides, if their technique could produce one such substance, it could probably produce others equally well.

Genentech produced its first genetically engineered human insulin in 1978. The substance was not actually marketed until

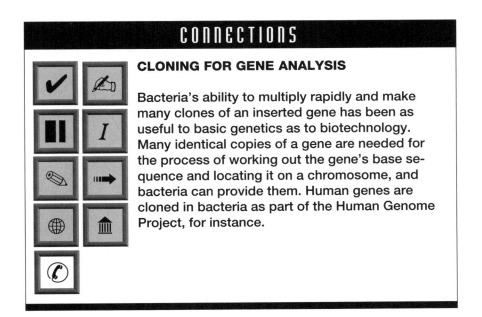

CONNECTIONS

CLONING FOR GENE ANALYSIS

Bacteria's ability to multiply rapidly and make many clones of an inserted gene has been as useful to basic genetics as to biotechnology. Many identical copies of a gene are needed for the process of working out the gene's base sequence and locating it on a chromosome, and bacteria can provide them. Human genes are cloned in bacteria as part of the Human Genome Project, for instance.

1982, however, partly because, like other medicines, this new form of the hormone had to gain the approval of the federal Food and Drug Administration (FDA) before being sold.

By 1981, 48 different human hormones were being made, at least experimentally, by genetically engineered bacteria. Other medically useful substances produced since then by gene-spliced microbes include tPA, a drug that helps to dissolve blood clots after heart attacks. Vaccines that protect people against diseases such as hepatitis B, a serious liver disease that can lead to cancer, have also been made by genetic engineering.

A Dangerous Test?

Medicine was not the only field that gained from genetic engineering. Some genetic engineers thought that even greater benefit—and profit—could be reaped from applying the new technology to farming. They began using gene splicing to do some of the things that farmers had done through breeding for centuries, such as developing plants that could resist disease or drought. They also attempted things that never would have been possible through breeding. Scientifically, many of these experiments succeeded. When researchers tried to take their products out of the laboratory, however, fear and controversy erupted, just as they had when genetic engineering was first used.

Steven Lindow, a young plant pathologist (a scientist who studies plant diseases) from the University of California at Berkeley, found out firsthand just how much trouble such controversy could cause. Lindow had discovered in 1975 that frost damage to crop plants, which cost farmers in the United States up to $1.5 billion a year, was greatly increased by the presence of a common bacterium called *Pseudomonas syringae*. These bacteria have a protein on their surface that is much like ice in structure. The protein encourages water molecules to solidify around it and form an ice crystal. Plants covered with *P. syringae* freeze at 32°

*Steve Lindow, a plant pathologist at the University of California at Berkeley, found
a way to use genetic engineering to alter bacteria that caused frost damage in plants.
He ran into trouble when he tried to test the engineered bacteria in open fields.*
(Courtesy Maria Brandl and the University of California at Berkeley)

F., while those from which the bacteria are removed remain
unfrozen until the temperature drops to 24° F.

There was no practical way to get rid of the bacteria, which are
found everywhere in soil, water, and air. Lindow found, however,
that some rare forms of *P. syringae* lacked the ability to help ice
form. These mutant bacteria proved to lack a single gene that the
normal type possessed. This had to be the gene that coded for the
ice-forming protein. If he could make more of these "ice-minus"
bacteria and spray them on plants, Lindow reasoned, they might
temporarily outcompete the normal form of the bacteria and
protect the plants against frost damage.

SOCIAL IMPACT

UNDERSTANDING RISK

People in Monterey County and Tulelake complained about what they saw as scientists' refusal to give them definite answers about the risks posed by Steve Lindow's tests. "[Their] words don't say yes or no," one farm worker said. "I thought the whole reason for that [environmental] impact report was to come up with yeses and noes." Science, however, can rarely say definitely that something will or will not happen. A 1988 report on the risks of genetic engineering by the U.S. Office of Technology Assessment stated:

> In evaluating the potential risks associated with these new technologies, the appropriate question is not "How can we reduce the potential risks to zero?" but "What are the relative risks of the new technologies compared with the risks of the technologies with which they will compete?" Furthermore, what are the risks posed by overregulating, or failing to develop fully the new technologies? How do we weigh costs and benefits?

Lindow and his coworkers used genetic engineering to remove the ice-forming gene from normal *Pseudomonas* bacteria. The resulting ice-minus bacteria were effective in greenhouse tests. In 1982, Lindow applied to the RAC for permission to test the genetically engineered bacteria in small fields owned by the university.

Before final approval was granted, however, genetic engineering foe Jeremy Rifkin found out about the proposed test. Noting that the test would be the first release of genetically engineered microorganisms into the environment, Rifkin persuaded several environmental groups to join him in opposing it.

Rifkin and his supporters, who included some scientists, feared that the ice-minus bacteria would spread out of their test fields and replace the normal, ice-creating form of *P. syringae*. This, they said, might upset the balance of ecosystems because plants would survive that would normally have been killed. Some scientists even thought that large amounts of ice-minus bacteria might change rainfall patterns. It was widely believed that *P. syringae* bacteria in the air helped rain occur by serving as nuclei for the formation of raindrops, and the ice-minus bacteria might not be able to do this.

For the next several years, questions from the RAC and lawsuits by Rifkin and his supporters trapped Lindow and his fellow researchers in ever-growing mazes of testing and paperwork. The scientists also had to try to calm public fears in Monterey County and Tulelake, the two California sites of the proposed tests. Nothing they said seemed to make any difference. Lindow complained to an interviewer,

> I'm afraid the public is so poorly educated in the scientific process, and about what scientists do, that they are susceptible to the kind of rhetoric [argument] that people like Rifkin would feed them. They are susceptible to emotional arguments. Most of the arguments against this are irrational.

Tulelake eventually agreed to let the tests take place, but Monterey County did not. The Monterey tests were moved to Contra Costa, another California county.

The ice-minus tests finally took place in the spring of 1987. The night before the tests, protesters broke into the fields and pulled up the strawberry plants in Contra Costa and the potato plants at Tulelake that were to be sprayed. The scientists replanted them, however, and the tests went forward. Results showed that the bacteria did protect the plants against frost and that they did not spread beyond the treated fields. "There were no surprises," Lindow reported.

New Items on the Deli Menu

Since those difficult days, a variety of genetically engineered products have come to be used or tested in agriculture. Some plants have been given genes from a bacterium, enabling them to make a poison that destroys pest insects without harming useful insects or other animals. Other crops have received genes that make them resistant to herbicides, chemicals sprayed on crops to kill weeds. A genetically engineered tomato that can be harvested ripe without damage was approved for use in human food and went on sale in 1992 under the name Flavr Savr. More recently, plants have been genetically altered to make them produce drugs or substances useful in industry.

During the late 1970s, genetic engineers also worked out ways to insert genes into the cells of mammals. By putting new genes into fertilized eggs, they created "transgenic" animals that ex-

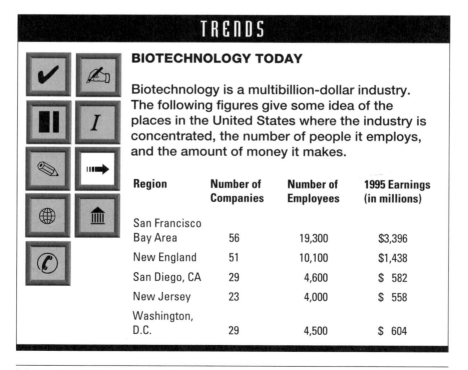

TRENDS

BIOTECHNOLOGY TODAY

Biotechnology is a multibillion-dollar industry. The following figures give some idea of the places in the United States where the industry is concentrated, the number of people it employs, and the amount of money it makes.

Region	Number of Companies	Number of Employees	1995 Earnings (in millions)
San Francisco Bay Area	56	19,300	$3,396
New England	51	10,100	$1,438
San Diego, CA	29	4,600	$ 582
New Jersey	23	4,000	$ 558
Washington, D.C.	29	4,500	$ 604

ISSUES

HAS BIOTECHNOLOGY BEEN OVERSOLD?

Even though almost 25 years have passed since the first genetic engineering experiments, relatively few biotechnology products have actually reached the marketplace. This slow progress has led some people to say that claims of wonderful things to come from genetic engineering have been greatly exaggerated. For example, Diane Beeson, a sociology professor at California State College at Hayward, says that the promised revolution to be brought about by genetic engineering "is still in the realm of fantasy. It's been grossly oversold." Only time will tell whether biotechnology will live up to its boosters' promises.

pressed genes from different species. Genes have been inserted, for example, to make cattle and pigs produce leaner meat and to make dairy cows give more milk. Other genes have made cattle or other mammals produce human hormones or other medically useful substances. Mice carrying human genes act as test animals for new treatments for AIDS and other diseases.

In February 1997, Ian Wilmut and other genetic engineers in Scotland startled the world by announcing that they had created a clone, or exact genetic duplicate, of a mammal from a single adult body cell for the first time. The group implanted DNA from a breast cell of a ewe (female sheep) into a fertilized sheep egg from which the egg's own DNA had been removed. They then placed the egg in the womb of another ewe, where it developed into a normal lamb. Tests show that the lamb, which the group named Dolly, has exactly the same genes as the sheep from which the breast cell came. Because of this achievement, the dream of cloning an adult human, which had seemed to belong to the realm of science fiction, suddenly seems quite possible. Cloning humans, of course, would raise many ethical issues.

The menu of items that can be ordered from the gene deli grows longer each year, and this growth is almost sure to continue. *Time* magazine wrote in 1981, "Gene splicing is the most powerful and awesome skill acquired by man since the splitting of the atom." Waclaw Szybalski of the University of Wisconsin at Madison added in 1985, "We've invented fire. The sky's the limit." Today, perhaps, the limit is not even the sky but outer space.

Chronology of Genetic Engineering

1972	Herbert Boyer and Stanley Cohen plan first gene-splicing project
1973	Paul Berg moves genes from one kind of virus to another; stops further experiments
	Boyer and Cohen move genes from one type of bacteria to another and show that the genes function in their new location
1974	Berg and other scientists suggest temporary halt to some gene-splicing experiments
1975	Meeting held at Asilomar, California, to work out safety guidelines for genetic engineering
	Steve Lindow discovers that frost damage in plants is increased by a common bacterium
1976	National Institutes of Health draws up standards based on those from Asilomar meeting
	Genentech founded
1980	NIH guidelines relaxed
	Genentech stock offered to public, sells wildly
1982	Genentech offers first product, human insulin
	Lindow applies for RAC permission to field-test ice-minus bacteria

1987	First genetically engineered microorganisms (ice-minus bacteria) released into environment
1992	Genetically engineered tomato marketed
February 1997	Scientists announce cloning of sheep from single adult cell

Further Reading

Baskin, Yvonne. "Getting the Bugs Out." *Atlantic Monthly*, June 1990. Describes Steven Lindow's research and his difficulties in gaining permission to release genetically altered microorganisms into the environment.

"The Biotech Chronicles." World Wide Web: http://www.gene.com/AE/AB/BC. Contains useful information about biotechnology, its background, and its key pioneers.

Filson, Brent. *Superconductors and Other New Breakthroughs in Science*. New York: Julian Messner, 1989. For young adults. Includes a chapter on ice-minus bacteria research and other advances in genetic engineering of microbes.

Golden, Frederick. "Shaping Life in the Lab." *Time*, March 9, 1981. Good overview article on early genetic engineering.

Golob, Richard, and Eric Brus, eds., *The Almanac of Science and Technology*. Boston: Harcourt Brace Jovanovich, 1990. Includes clear description of basic process of genetic engineering, how it began, and some advances in the field.

Hall, Stephen S. "One Potato Patch That Is Making Genetic History." *Smithsonian*, August 1987. Describes Steven Lindow's research, his proposed tests of ice-minus bacteria, and their importance in genetic engineering.

Miller, Julie Ann. "Lessons from Asilomar." *Science News*, February 23, 1985. Ten years after the Asilomar meeting, scientists evaluate the meeting's conclusions.

NOTES

p. 63   "Well, now we can put together . . ." Quoted in Edward Shorter. *The Health Century* (New York: Doubleday, 1987), p. 238.

p. 65   "Most of the work . . ." Quoted in N. A. Tiley, *Discovering DNA* (New York: Van Nostrand Reinhold, 1993), p. 258.

p. 66   "a new era . . ." Quoted in Joel Gurin and Nancy E. Pfund. "Bonanza in the Bio Lab," *Nation*, Nov. 22, 1980, p. 544.

p. 68   "the most spectacular . . ." Quoted in Gurin and Pfund, p. 548.

p. 72   "[Their] words . . ." Quoted in Hall, pp. 126, 128.

p. 72   "In evaluating . . ." Quoted in Yvonne Baskin. "Getting the Bugs Out," *Atlantic Monthly*, June 1990, p. 47.

p. 73   "I'm afraid the public . . ." Quoted in Stephen S. Hall. "One Potato Patch that Is Making Genetic History," *Smithsonian*, August 1987, p. 133.

p. 73   "There were no . . ." Quoted in Thomas H. Maugh, III. "Biotech Bugs Leave the Lab—at Last," *Discover*, January 1988, p. 84.

p. 75   "is still in the realm . . ." Quoted in Keay Davidson. "Genes Don't Fit the Hype, Say DNA Skeptics," *San Francisco Examiner*, September 22, 1996.

p. 76   "Gene splicing is . . ." Quoted in Frederic Golden. "Shaping Life in the Lab," *Time*, March 9, 1981, p. 50.

p. 76   "We've invented fire . . ." Quoted in Julie Ann Miller. "Lessons from Asilomar," *Science News*, February 23, 1985, p. 123.

5

The Enemy Within

MICHAEL BISHOP, HAROLD VARMUS,
AND GENES THAT CAUSE CANCER

*Michael Bishop and other scientists at the University of California at
San Francisco showed that mutated forms of normal genes can cause
cancer.* (Courtesy Mikkel Aaland and the University of California at
San Francisco)

Cancer is one of humanity's most frightening diseases. It has been known as a killer since ancient times. The Romans named it after their word for *crab*, perhaps from the shape of the masses of multiplying cells, or tumors, that often characterize the disease. Until this century the only cure for cancer was to remove or destroy the tumor, and that only worked sometimes. Often the disease spread and formed new tumors elsewhere in the body, eventually causing death. The cause of the disease was completely unknown.

Until the 1970s, 20th-century scientists knew only that cancers consisted of cells that multiplied wildly. As their number grew, cancer cells pushed against or otherwise damaged normal cells. The result was pain, destruction of tissues and organs, and often death. The behavior of cancer cells was very different from that of most normal cells, which multiplied only at certain stages of a living thing's development. Cancer seemed to defy the pattern of development built into each organism's genes.

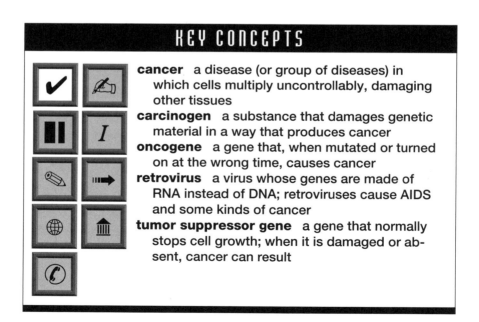

KEY CONCEPTS

cancer   a disease (or group of diseases) in which cells multiply uncontrollably, damaging other tissues

carcinogen   a substance that damages genetic material in a way that produces cancer

oncogene   a gene that, when mutated or turned on at the wrong time, causes cancer

retrovirus   a virus whose genes are made of RNA instead of DNA; retroviruses cause AIDS and some kinds of cancer

tumor suppressor gene   a gene that normally stops cell growth; when it is damaged or absent, cancer can result

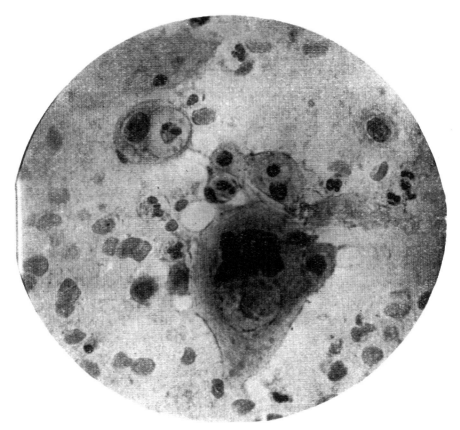

Cancer cells like those in the center of this picture multiply uncontrollably, damaging nearby tissues. (Courtesy American Cancer Society)

A Cancer-Causing Virus

The first hint about what makes cancer cells "go bad" came from sick chickens. In 1910 a farmer brought a chicken with a breast tumor to the laboratory of Francis Peyton Rous, a researcher at the Rockefeller Institute for Medical Research in New York City. The farmer told Rous that other chickens in his flock also had tumors. This kind of cancer seemed to be contagious, as if it were caused by a microbe.

Curious, Rous broke up cells from the tumor and forced the mixture through filters small enough to remove even the tiniest bacteria. He then injected the filtered material into a healthy chicken. It developed a tumor. Rous concluded that the chicken cancer must be caused by a virus. At that time, no one had ever seen viruses. Scientists used that name for organisms that, they theorized, were smaller than bacteria. Certain diseases, such as rabies, were blamed on viruses. No one had ever suggested that a virus could cause cancer, though. Indeed, one researcher told Rous, "Look here, young man, that can't be a cancer if you've found its cause." Still, time and further experiments proved Rous to be right. He won a Nobel Prize for his work in 1966, when he was 87 years old.

In the early 1970s, scientists found that DNA from cells infected by what had come to be called the Rous sarcoma virus (a sarcoma is one kind of cancer tumor) could make normal cells in laboratory dishes begin acting like cancer cells. This was also true

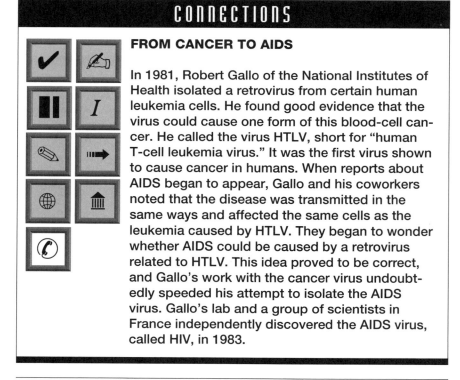

CONNECTIONS

FROM CANCER TO AIDS

In 1981, Robert Gallo of the National Institutes of Health isolated a retrovirus from certain human leukemia cells. He found good evidence that the virus could cause one form of this blood-cell cancer. He called the virus HTLV, short for "human T-cell leukemia virus." It was the first virus shown to cause cancer in humans. When reports about AIDS began to appear, Gallo and his coworkers noted that the disease was transmitted in the same ways and affected the same cells as the leukemia caused by HTLV. They began to wonder whether AIDS could be caused by a retrovirus related to HTLV. This idea proved to be correct, and Gallo's work with the cancer virus undoubtedly speeded his attempt to isolate the AIDS virus. Gallo's lab and a group of scientists in France independently discovered the AIDS virus, called HIV, in 1983.

of cells infected by several other viruses that produced cancers in animals. Unlike most viruses, cancer-causing viruses did not kill the cells they occupied. Instead, they stayed in the cells and altered them profoundly.

A discovery made by David Baltimore of the Whitehead Institute for Biomedical Research in Cambridge, Massachusetts, in 1970 showed how cancer-causing viruses did their dirty work. Baltimore found that, unlike that of other living things, these viruses' genetic material is made of RNA rather than DNA. When the viruses inject their RNA into cells, a unique chemical called reverse transcriptase performs the usual genetic operation backwards: instead of transcribing DNA into RNA, it forms a DNA copy of the virus's RNA genes. This DNA is then inserted into the cells' genes, where it is copied in the normal way, producing more viruses. In effect, these "backwards" viruses, or retroviruses, do their own gene splicing. They are nature's genetic engineers.

Genes That Cause Cancer

Researchers in the early 1970s found a form of the Rous sarcoma retrovirus that had lost its power to cause cancer. They analyzed the genes of this harmless form to see how they differed from those of the cancer-causing type. The cancer-causing form of the virus, it developed, had one large gene at the end of its tiny genome that the harmless form lacked. Somehow, that gene must cause cancer. The researchers gave it the name *src*, for sarcoma. Other scientists found different cancer-causing genes in other viruses.

Robert Huebner and George Todaro of the National Cancer Institute, part of the National Institutes of Health, gave all these genes the name *oncogenes*, after a Greek word meaning "cancer." They proposed that tumor viruses slipped oncogenes into cells much as a terrorist might smuggle in a bomb to blow up a building or a plane.

Harold Varmus (shown here) met Michael Bishop almost by accident and joined him in the cancer research that won both scientists a Nobel Prize in 1989.
(Courtesy Karen Preuss and the University of California at San Francisco)

This genetic "bomb," however, might not go off for centuries. Huebner and Todaro suggested that normal cell genomes contained potential oncogenes—what they called proviruses—left over from viral infection in the distant evolutionary past. These proviruses were passed on to descendants along with the living thing's normal genes. They became active and caused cancer only if triggered by exposure to agents such as X rays or certain chemicals. When two scientists at the University of California at San Francisco (UCSF) tried to test the provirus theory in 1972, however, they ended up standing Huebner and Todaro's idea on its head. They found that oncogenes, rather than being introduced into cells originally by viruses, had first gotten into viruses from the cells they infected.

That Michael Bishop and Harold Varmus should make such a surprising discovery was something of a surprise in itself: in his early years, neither man had dreamed that he would become a scientist. Born in York, Pennsylvania, in 1936, Bishop had been interested primarily in music. Varmus, born in 1939 in Oceanside, New York, earned a master's degree in English literature. Both eventually turned to medical research, though. Varmus came to San Francisco and met Bishop "almost by accident." He recalls that "Mike and I hit it off right away," just as James Watson and

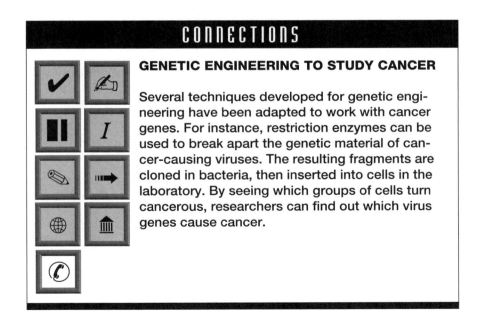

CONNECTIONS

GENETIC ENGINEERING TO STUDY CANCER

Several techniques developed for genetic engineering have been adapted to work with cancer genes. For instance, restriction enzymes can be used to break apart the genetic material of cancer-causing viruses. The resulting fragments are cloned in bacteria, then inserted into cells in the laboratory. By seeing which groups of cells turn cancerous, researchers can find out which virus genes cause cancer.

Francis Crick did when they met at Cambridge. Varmus joined Bishop's laboratory at UCSF in 1970.

Dominique Stehelin, a French researcher working with Bishop and Varmus, used reverse transcriptase, the viral chemical David Baltimore had discovered, to make copies of the *src* gene from the Rous sarcoma virus. He labeled the genes with a radioactive tracer and then mixed them with DNA from the cells of normal chickens. If a form of *src*—a provirus—existed in the DNA of the chicken cells, the labeled *src* would stick to it and mark its location.

In 1976, the researchers succeeded in finding a gene similar to *src* in healthy chicken cells. To their amazement, further analysis showed that this *src*-like gene had the form of a cell gene, not a virus gene. They also found that the gene was active in the cells, even though the cells were not cancerous. In other words, *src*, or a gene almost identical to it, apparently was—or had been—a normal chicken gene. Before tumor viruses became terrorists, it seemed, they had been thieves, taking a killer gene from the cells themselves. Bishop and Varmus called the normal form of *src* a cellular oncogene because the cell gene, like the viral form, could cause cancer under the right circumstances.

That was just the beginning of the surprises. Another researcher in Bishop's lab, Deborah Spector, found versions of *src* in fish, birds, mammals—and humans. This meant that the gene had remained the same throughout a long period of evolution. That would not have happened unless the gene did something very basic and important in cells. "Cancer may be part of the genetic dowry [inheritance] of every living cell," Michael Bishop has said.

Bishop and Varmus received a Nobel Prize in 1989 for their discovery. "[Their] work gave us a new way of thinking about cancer," David Baltimore told an interviewer. "Until they made their discoveries, there was only speculation that cancer had a genetic component. Now there is a certainty." Other oncogenes found originally in viruses have also proved to be altered forms of normal cell genes. Scientists today know of more than 50 such genes.

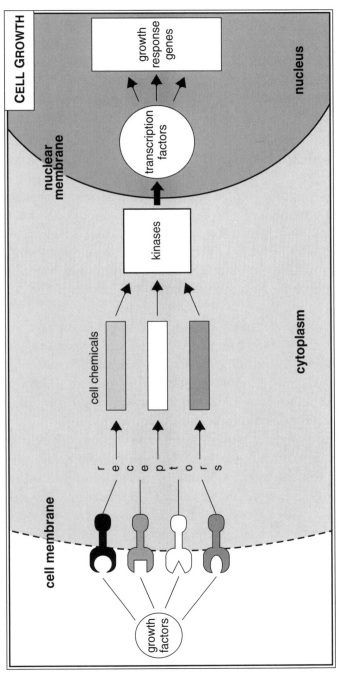

CELL GROWTH

Cell growth is triggered by a complicated chain of chemical signals. The signaling begins with chemicals called growth factors, which come to the cell from other cells, and ends in the cell nucleus, where genes that cause the cell to divide are turned on. Other links in the chain include receptors in the cell membrane, to which the growth factors attach; different kinds of chemicals in the cytoplasm, or cell body; kinases, activated by these chemicals, which in turn activate chemicals that can enter the cell nucleus; and transcription factors, which turn on the genes that make the cell divide. Changes in any of the proteins in the chain can result in faulty signals that lead to the uncontrolled growth of cancer. Such changes result from mutations in the genes that makes the proteins.

How Oncogenes Work

Cellular oncogenes, like other genes, make proteins. Finding out what these proteins do in the cell was the next task researchers faced. Around 1980, Bishop and Varmus and another group of researchers at the University of Colorado discovered independently that *src* made a cell chemical called a protein kinase. Kinases add phosphate groups to certain amino acids in proteins. This process, called phosphorylation, changes the proteins greatly. It is essential for a variety of vital cell activities, especially those connected with growth. Several kinds of oncogenes have turned out to make kinases that phosphorylate different groups of proteins. Normally, kinases work only when they receive signals from certain other cell chemicals. When the oncogenes are in their cancer-causing form, though, their kinases are active all the time.

Researchers found that the normal forms of other oncogenes carry out equally important functions. Some, for instance, produce proteins called growth factors, which make cells grow and multiply. These genes are supposed to be turned on only at certain times. In their cancer-causing form, however, they produce growth-enhancing proteins constantly.

Other oncogenes make proteins called receptors, to which growth-promoting substances attach. When a growth substance links onto a receptor, the receptor sends signals to kinases or other substances in the cell, producing growth. Receptors made by the cancer-causing form of oncogenes act as if they are receiving growth-promoting substances all the time.

Cancer researchers also learned several different ways in which a cellular oncogene changes to its cancer-causing form. One way involves a mutation in one or more base pairs of the gene. In 1981, Robert Weinberg of the Whitehead Institute found an oncogene called *ras* in a human bladder tumor. This was the first oncogene isolated from a human cancer. When Weinberg and his coworkers analyzed the normal and cancer-causing forms of the *ras* gene,

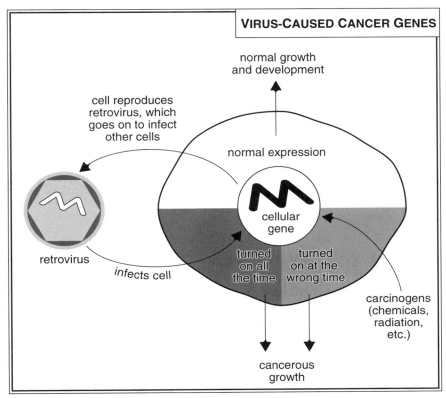

VIRUS-CAUSED CANCER GENES

normal growth
and development

cell reproduces
retrovirus, which
goes on to infect
other cells

normal expression

cellular
gene

retrovirus

infects cell

turned
on all
the time

turned
on at the
wrong time

carcinogens
(chemicals,
radiation,
etc.)

cancerous
growth

When a retrovirus infects a cell, it sometimes inserts a gene, called an oncogene, that makes the cell become cancerous. Michael Bishop and Harold Varmus found that such genes came originally from other cells that the viruses infected long ago. Carcinogens—cancer-causing substances in the environment—can also change a normal cell gene into an oncogene. In both cases, the oncogene differs from the normal form of the same gene in that the oncogene either produces its protein all the time or produces it at the wrong time in the cell's life cycle.

they found that the two differed by only one base pair. This tiny difference was enough to cause major changes in the gene's action.

In other cases, the scientists found, a cellular oncogene becomes able to cause cancer when it is moved from one chromosome, or one spot on a chromosome, to another. This can happen, for example, during the chromosome breakage and rejoining that occurs in crossing over. The move may place the oncogene next to a gene that signals it to turn on.

A cellular oncogene can also be turned on at the wrong time when stretches of DNA called promoters are inserted before and after it. Sometimes these promoter sequences come from cancer-causing viruses. In other cases, movement of genes or chromosome parts within a cell places a cellular oncogene between promoter sequences. In either case, the promoters push the oncogene into a high level of activity. A third way of activating cellular oncogenes is through gene amplification, in which extra copies of a gene are accidentally made. All these copies can make protein, so the result is a larger-than-normal amount of the gene's protein.

An Opposite of Oncogenes

As if oncogenes were not enough, scientists in the early 1980s discovered a second type of gene that can play a role in starting cancer. These genes are the exact opposite of oncogenes: instead of producing cell growth, their normal job is stopping it. They cause cancer, not when they become overactive as happens with oncogenes, but when they fail to function. Cancer researchers call these genes tumor suppressor genes. If active oncogenes are like a stuck accelerator on a car, missing tumor suppressor genes are the equivalent of defective brakes.

Researchers found the first tumor suppressor gene in a rare type of cancer that strikes young children. This cancer, called retinoblastoma, grows in the eye. Doctors usually have to remove one or both eyes in order to save the child's life. Sometimes the genetic damage that causes this kind of tumor is inherited, but in other cases it is not.

As Gregor Mendel discovered, a living thing inherits two copies of each gene, one from its father and one from its mother. Both copies affect the same protein or characteristic but may or may not have the same form. One form of a certain pea plant gene produces tallness and a different form of the same gene produces shortness, for instance. In 1971, researcher Alfred G. Knudson,

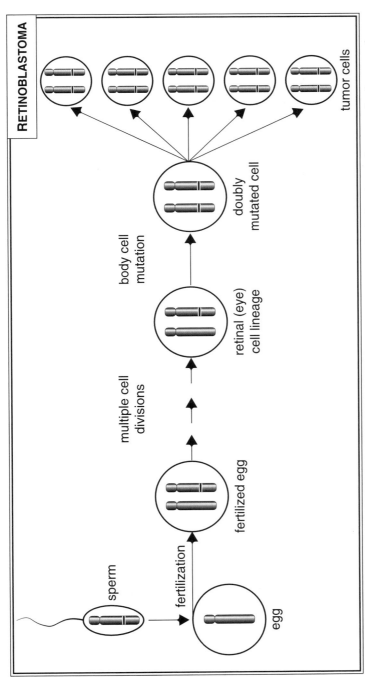

RETINOBLASTOMA

sperm

fertilization

egg

fertilized egg

multiple cell divisions

retinal (eye) cell lineage

body cell mutation

doubly mutated cell

tumor cells

The damaged genes that result in the eye cancer called retinoblastoma are sometimes inherited and sometimes not. In the example here, a child inherits one damaged gene (horizontal bar) from its father. If a mutation damages the healthy gene (inherited from the mother) while eye cells are multiplying before birth—an event fairly likely to happen—the cell in which the mutation occurs will lose the power to control its growth. It will multiply and form a tumor. A tumor can also result if both copies of the gene are normal when inherited from the parents but become damaged before birth.

OTHER SCIENTISTS

THEODORE DRYJA AND RETINOBLASTOMA

Theodore Dryja, a doctor at the Massachusetts Eye and Ear Hospital in Boston, did much of the work of locating the retinoblastoma gene.

Dryja had all too often had the painful task of removing eyes from children with retinoblastoma. Although untrained in molecular biology, he wanted to take part in the hunt for the gene that caused this disease. He taught himself what he needed to know. Once scientists showed that the gene was on chromosome 13, Dryja patiently began cloning bits of the chromosome and testing them against DNA from both normal eye cells and retinoblastoma cells. One day in 1986 he finally found a DNA sequence that was present in normal cells but missing in retinoblastoma. "I couldn't sleep for a week after I saw that," he said later. He turned his DNA samples over to Robert Weinberg's better-equipped laboratory, where the actual isolation of the gene was done.

Jr., proposed that both copies of some gene, then unknown, had to be defective in order to produce retinoblastoma. Some children, he said, inherited one faulty copy of the gene and later lost the second copy through random mutation, perhaps when eye cells multiplied rapidly before birth. In other, rarer cases, a child inherited two normal genes but mutations made both of them inactive. If this occurred in even one cell, that cell would begin multiplying uncontrollably and produce a tumor.

But what gene was missing? Jorge Yunis of the University of Minnesota Medical School got a clue when he found that a part of chromosome 13 was missing in all the cells of children with inherited retinoblastoma but only in the tumor cells of those with the noninherited form of the disease. Using genetic engineering techniques similar to those that had helped Bishop and Varmus find the *src* gene, several sets of scientists began searching that part of the chromosome for a gene that suppressed cell growth. The gene, called *Rb* for retinoblastoma, was finally located in 1986 by Stephen H. Friend in Robert Weinberg's laboratory. This gene has since been found in a variety of tissues, and it has proved to be missing in several different kinds of cancer.

Since that time, a number of other tumor suppressor genes have been found. One, called p53, has proved to be mutated or absent in a wide variety of cancers, including colon, bladder, and breast cancer. Indeed, a mutation that inactivates p53's protein "occurs in maybe half the total cancers in the United States," says cancer researcher Bert Vogelstein of Johns Hopkins University. Unlike the case with *Rb*, even a single defective copy of p53 can result in a defective protein and loss of the ability to suppress growth.

As with growth-promoting genes, the proteins made by tumor suppressor genes are parts of a chain of signals that tell a cell what to do. A break or change in any link of the chain can keep the whole chain from functioning normally. Some tumor suppressor proteins have been found to interact with the growth-promoting proteins produced by oncogenes.

A Multistep Process

Researchers have learned that more than one change in genes almost always is required to start a cancer. In the late 1980s, for instance, Bert Vogelstein found that at least four different mutations—activation of one oncogene and inactivation of three growth suppressor genes, including p53—are required to produce a cancer in the colon (large intestine). If cancer were a gun, the first mutation would put a bullet in the chamber, the second take the safety off, the third cock the trigger, and the fourth fire the weapon. These changes may occur years apart and arise from different causes. That is why it usually takes many years for a cancer to develop and why most cancers occur in older people.

Sometimes potential cancer-causing mutations enter the genes of the reproductive cells and are passed on to offspring, giving the

SOCIAL IMPACT

CANCER AND CIGARETTES

Many cancers are the result of lifestyle choices, such as deciding to smoke cigarettes. A strong statistical link between tobacco smoking and certain cancers, especially lung cancer, has been known for some time, but scientists had not been able to show exactly how tobacco smoke caused cancer. In October 1996, however, scientists from Texas and California showed that a chemical in tobacco smoke damages the p53 tumor suppressor gene in lung cells. This same kind of damage is found in many lung tumors. John Minna, a researcher at the University of Texas, says, "This paper absolutely pinpoints that mutations in lung cancer are caused by a carcinogen in cigarette smoke."

offspring an increased risk of cancer. This is why certain kinds of cancer, like some forms of retinoblastoma, "run in families." In other cases, environmental factors damage genes in particular body cells during an individual's lifespan. Cells have ways to repair such damage, but if unrepaired changes occur in even a single cell, a tumor may start.

Most of the time, both heredity and environment play a role in starting cancer. A person might inherit one kind of mutated gene, for instance, but will not develop a tumor unless a second or even a third gene is damaged by environmental factors. Environment, however, is more important than heredity in causing most cancers. A report prepared by the U.S. Office of Technology Assessment in the early 1980s estimated that about 80 percent of deaths from cancer in the United States were caused by smoking, diet, or other environmental or lifestyle factors.

Cancer-causing viruses are one kind of environmental factor that can produce genetic changes. Only a small number of human cancers appear to be caused by viruses, however. Most cancers in people result from damage caused by high-energy radiation, such as X rays or sunlight, or by certain chemicals. Chemicals that can change normal cells into cancerous ones are called carcinogens. Carcinogens are found in tobacco smoke, smog, and many other substances in the environment. They have in common an ability to change or damage DNA in cells, causing a great increase in mutations. If these mutations occur in or indirectly affect cellular oncogenes or tumor suppressor genes, cancer may be the result. Michael Bishop has called these genes "the keyboard on which carcinogens play."

Cancer researcher Tony Hunter of the Salk Institute in La Jolla, California, has said, "As complicated as we think things are" in cancer research, "they're sure to be more complicated than that." No matter how complex the picture of cancer causation becomes, however, the basic truth is the one that Michael Bishop and Harold Varmus first uncovered more than 20 years ago: the secret of cancer lies in the genes. Although viruses, carcinogens, or other environmental factors may trigger it, this terrible disease ultimately is not an attack by an outside enemy but a crazed revolt within our own bodies. As Michael Bishop has said, "We carry the seeds of our cancer within us."

Chronology of Genetic Cancer Research

1910	Peyton Rous theorizes that a virus can cause cancer
1936	J. Michael Bishop born in York, Pennsylvania
1939	Harold Varmus born in Oceanside, New York
1970	David Baltimore discovers reverse transcriptase in retroviruses
	Varmus joins Bishop's lab at UCSF
early 1970s	Robert Huebner and George Todaro theorize that cancer comes from oncogenes left behind by viruses
1976	Bishop and Varmus find normal cell gene that resembles oncogene, theorize that oncogenes came originally from cells

1981	Robert Weinberg finds oncogene in a human cancer
1986	Stephen Friend isolates defective tumor suppressor gene from human eye tumor
late 1980s	Bert Vogelstein finds that four mutations are needed to produce colon cancer
1989	Bishop and Varmus win Nobel Prize
October 1996	Scientists pinpoint specific cancer-causing damage done by tobacco smoke

Further Reading

Angier, Natalie. *Natural Obsessions*. New York: Warner Books, 1988. Excellent book on breakthroughs in cancer research in the 1970s and 1980s. Focuses on Robert Weinberg's laboratory but includes information on Bishop and Varmus.

Baltimore, David. "Conquering the Gene." *Discover*, October 1989. Describes oncogenes and other aspects of cancer first discovered in the 1970s and 1980s.

"The Biotech Chronicles." World Wide Web: http://www.gene.com./AE/AB/BC. Short biographies of Bishop and Varmus are obtainable through this source.

Bishop, J. Michael. "Oncogenes." *Scientific American*, March 1982. Describes nature and discovery of oncogenes. Somewhat difficult reading.

Marx, Jean L. "Cancer Gene Research Wins Medicine Nobel." *Science*, October 20, 1989. Describes the cancer research that won Bishop and Varmus a Nobel Prize.

Varmus, Harold, and Robert A. Weinberg. *Genes and the Biology of Cancer*. New York: Scientific American Library, 1993. Interesting, well-illustrated books describes recent discoveries in cancer biology at the cellular level.

Wallis, Claudia. "Advances in the War on Cancer." *Time*, November 8, 1982. Describes discoveries of Bishop, Varmus, and Weinberg in cancer genetics.

Yount, Lisa. *Cancer*. San Diego, Calif.: Lucent Books, 1991. For young adults. Overview of cancer's causes and treatment, including recent research in the field.

NOTES

p. 82   "Look here . . ." Quoted in Walter Bodmer and Robin McKie. *The Book of Man* (New York: Scribner, 1994), p. 95.

p. 85   "almost by accident." Quoted in Jean L. Marx. "Cancer Gene Research Wins Medicine Nobel," *Science*, October 20, 1989, p. 326.

p. 86   "Cancer may be part . . ." Quoted in Claudia Wallis. "Advances in the War on Cancer," *Time*, November 8, 1982, p. 70.

p. 86   "[Their] work . . ." Quoted in A. McKenzie. "Gene-Tracking Leads to Nobel Prize," *Science News*, October 7, 1989, p. 244.

p. 92   "I couldn't sleep . . ." Quoted in Natalie Angier. *Natural Obsessions* (New York: Warner Books, 1988), p. 337.

p. 93   "occurs in maybe half . . ." Quoted in Lisa Yount. *Cancer* (San Diego: Lucent Books, 1991), p. 85.

p. 94   "This paper absolutely . . ." Quoted in David Stout. "Tobacco, Cancer Linked at Cell Level," *New York Times*, reprinted in *San Francisco Chronicle*, October 18, 1996.

p. 95   "the keyboard . . ." Quoted in Marx, p. 327.

p. 95   "As complicated . . ." Quoted in Angier, p. 311.

p. 95   "We carry . . ." Quoted in Angier, p. 67.

6

Death in the family

NANCY WEXLER AND THE SEARCH FOR DISEASE-CAUSING GENES

Nancy Wexler has been a leader in research to discover the gene that causes Huntington's disease, which took her mother's life and threatens her own. (Courtesy Rob Marinissen and the Hereditary Disease Foundation)

98

. . . .

Imagine you're 22 years old. You have just finished a year of graduate study abroad. Then one day your father asks you to come home. When you arrive, he tells you and your older sister that your mother is suffering from an incurable brain disease. It "runs in her family"; her father and three brothers died of it. After 10 or 15 years of slow degeneration, she will die, too. You and your sister each have a 50-50 chance of someday meeting the same fate.

Most people would be devastated by an experience like this. They might have a breakdown or even consider suicide. When Nancy Wexler lived through this scene in August 1968, however, she reacted differently. After her first shock and grief wore off, she decided to fight against the disease that threatened her family. "She went from being dismal to being challenged and wanting to be a knight in shining armor going out to fight the devils," recalls her father, Milton Wexler, a Los Angeles psychoanalyst.

A Deadly Legacy

Wexler and the girls' mother, Leonore, had divorced four years earlier, but Leonore told him about her problems because she still considered him a friend. She told him about the police officer who had accused her of being drunk because she staggered when she crossed a street. She told him when a doctor finally found out what was really wrong with her: Huntington's disease.

Named after George Huntington, the doctor who first described it in 1872, this inherited disease affects about 30,000 people in the United States. It causes depression, bursts of anger or violence, memory loss, confusion, and shaking movements that, as the disease advances, grow into a grotesque, writhing "dance" that never stops. All these effects result from destruction of small but vital areas of the brain called the basal ganglia, a destruction masterminded by a single dominant gene. Huntington's disease is one of about 4,000 human diseases known to be inherited. Such diseases affect 15 million people in the United States.

There is no cure or even treatment for this relentless disease. Perhaps most tragic of all, signs of it usually do not appear until a person is 30 or 40 years old. By then, many of its victims have had children. A person who carries the Huntington's gene has a 50-50 chance of passing it on to each offspring. Because the gene is dominant, anyone who inherits it will develop the disease.

Milton Wexler, like his daughter, was a fighter. In addition to seeing to Leonore's care, he learned everything about Huntington's disease that he could. He also contacted Marjorie Guthrie, widow of the disease's most famous victim, folk singer Woody Guthrie. Guthrie had died of Huntington's in 1967. Soon afterward, Marjorie Guthrie had founded an organization called the Committee to Combat Huntington's Chorea (an older name for the disease). After meeting with Guthrie, Wexler opened a new chapter of her group in Los Angeles, where he lived.

Nancy Wexler did the same in Michigan, where she started that fall on a doctoral program in psychology at the University of

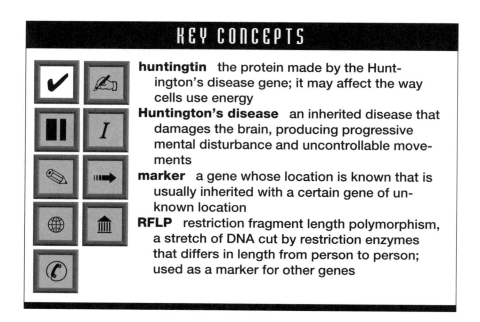

KEY CONCEPTS

huntingtin the protein made by the Huntington's disease gene; it may affect the way cells use energy

Huntington's disease an inherited disease that damages the brain, producing progressive mental disturbance and uncontrollable movements

marker a gene whose location is known that is usually inherited with a certain gene of unknown location

RFLP restriction fragment length polymorphism, a stretch of DNA cut by restriction enzymes that differs in length from person to person; used as a marker for other genes

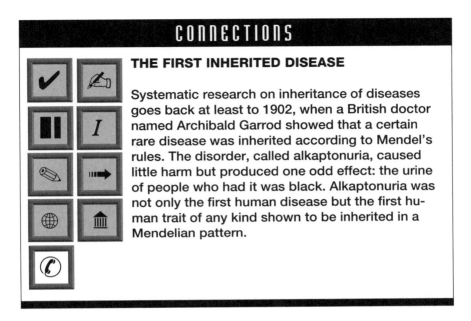

CONNECTIONS

THE FIRST INHERITED DISEASE

Systematic research on inheritance of diseases goes back at least to 1902, when a British doctor named Archibald Garrod showed that a certain rare disease was inherited according to Mendel's rules. The disorder, called alkaptonuria, caused little harm but produced one odd effect: the urine of people who had it was black. Alkaptonuria was not only the first human disease but the first human trait of any kind shown to be inherited in a Mendelian pattern.

Michigan at Ann Arbor. Drawing on her own experiences and those of other members of Huntington's families she met, she wrote her Ph.D. thesis on the mental and emotional effects of being a member of such a family. She received her doctor's degree in 1974.

Marjorie Guthrie's organization focused on finding better ways to care for people with Huntington's disease. Milton Wexler was more interested in searching for a cure. In 1974 he broke away from Guthrie's group and formed his own organization, the Hereditary Disease Foundation. From the start, Nancy was a key part of this group.

Needle in a Genetic Haystack

Several times each year, the Hereditary Disease Foundation invites scientists interested in Huntington's research to a combination seminar and party. "We ask for . . . people's imagination, energy, and affection for a weekend," Nancy Wexler has said. Ideas that might be too experimental for more formal scientific gatherings are welcome there.

David Housman of the Massachusetts Institute of Technology (MIT) brought up just such an idea at a meeting in October 1979. He and the other researchers knew that the best thing they could do to combat Huntington's would be to find the gene that caused it. Such a discovery would produce a test for the disease, which would allow people to find out whether they carried the dangerous gene before they had children. It also could lead to a better understanding of the illness and, possibly, a treatment or even cure for it. Finding one gene among a human's 100,000, when researchers had no idea which chromosome it was on or what protein it made, seemed far harder than hunting the proverbial needle in a haystack. Still, Housman had heard of a new technique that just might do the job.

The technique used restriction enzymes, those same molecular scissors that had proven so invaluable in genetic engineering. Molecular biologists had found that, because genes differ slightly in length and composition from person to person, a particular restriction enzyme did not snip everyone's DNA into pieces of exactly the same size. A fragment from a certain chromosome in Person A might be 12,000 base pairs long, for instance, while the equivalent fragment from Person B might be 13,500 base pairs long. Researchers had identified a number of spots where these inherited differences showed up. They called them restriction fragment length polymorphisms (polymorphism means "something having many forms"), or RFLPs for short. They pronounced this abbreviation "riflips."

Housman explained that RFLPs could be used as markers for other genes that were as yet unknown, like signposts on a road. If a particular form of RFLP was always or almost always inherited along with a certain gene, that gene was almost sure to lie very close to the RFLP on a chromosome. If analysis of a person's DNA showed that he or she had inherited the form of the RFLP that was associated with that gene, then the person very probably had inherited the gene as well. (The conclusion could never be

PARALLELS

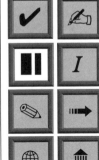

GENE MAPS OLD AND NEW

The scientists looking for a marker for the Huntington's gene had a tool that Thomas Hunt Morgan and his coworkers in Columbia University's Fly Room had lacked: restriction enzymes that cut DNA molecules in particular spots. They also had a knowledge of DNA's structure and function that had not existed in Morgan's time. Nonetheless, the RFLP technique they used was based on the same two phenomena that let Alfred Sturtevant make the first chromosome map in Morgan's laboratory. One was the fact that genes usually inherited together are close together on the same chromosome (linkage). The other was the process in which chromosomes break apart and then rejoin during formation of sex cells (crossing over or recombination).

completely certain because it was always possible that a chromosome break had fallen between the RFLP and the gene, separating the two.)

The problem with looking for the Huntington's gene by studying RFLPs was that no one knew where to start. At the time Housman told his fellow scientists about the procedure, only one human RFLP marker was known. Skeptics thought it might take 50 years or more to find a RFLP that was linked with the Huntington's gene—if, indeed, it ever happened at all.

Still, the RFLP idea was better than anything anyone else had thought of. The Hereditary Disease Foundation agreed to provide a grant for the work. Nancy Wexler arranged for further funding through the Congressional Commission for the Control of Huntington's Disease and Its Consequences, of which she had been made executive director in 1976.

Visit to Venezuela

The first thing Housman and his coworkers would need for their research was a large family containing members who had Huntington's. The family had to be large because many members, both sick and healthy, would have to be tested in order to establish that a particular form of a RFLP was consistently inherited with the gene that caused the disease. Fortunately, genetics researchers around the world had begun keeping records of families in which particular inherited disease occurred. Housman's group learned that the largest American family with Huntington's lived in Iowa. They also were told about a far bigger Huntington's family in Venezuela, on the shores of a large lake called Maracaibo.

As it happened, Nancy Wexler had known about the Venezuelan family since 1972. Indeed, pursuing a different question about the inheritance of the disease, she had visited them earlier in 1979.

It was a remarkable experience. Accompanied by a group of other American and Venezuelan scientists, Wexler had found members of the family living in three villages: San Luis, Barranquitas, and Laguneta. San Luis was a poverty-stricken settlement on the outskirts of the city of Maracaibo. Barranquitas was several hours' drive away. The third settlement, Laguneta, could be reached only by boat. Wexler and the others found the brightly colored houses in this little fishing village standing on stiltlike pilings above the marshy waters of the lake.

Practically the first person Wexler saw in Laguneta was a skeletally thin woman hunched in the doorway of one of the stilt houses. When an expedition member spoke to her, the woman spread her arms and began a writhing motion that Wexler recognized all too well. Wexler later told an interviewer,

> It was so amazing to me. Here I was in the middle of nowhere, palm trees all around, houses built over the water on stilts. Yet, here was a person who looked exactly like Mom. To be in someplace so alien and see something so familiar at the same time—that was just breathtaking.

Huntington's disease was so common among this Venezuelan family that family members simply accepted it as part of their hard life. They called it *el mal*—"the sickness" or "the bad thing." Even some children had the disease.

Blood, Skin, and DNA

When the RFLP work was ready to start in 1981, Wexler returned to Venezuela to collect blood and skin samples from family members for DNA testing. (Later on, blood alone was used.) At first Wexler's group had trouble explaining to the Venezuelans

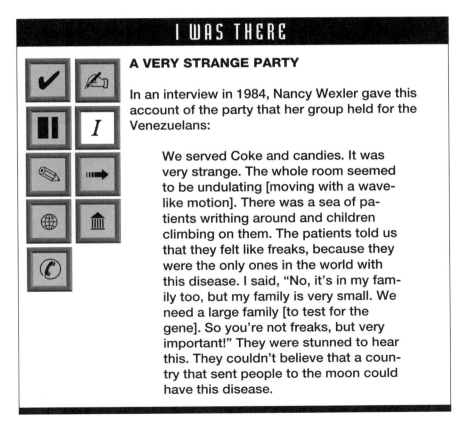

I WAS THERE

A VERY STRANGE PARTY

In an interview in 1984, Nancy Wexler gave this account of the party that her group held for the Venezuelans:

> We served Coke and candies. It was very strange. The whole room seemed to be undulating [moving with a wave-like motion]. There was a sea of patients writhing around and children climbing on them. The patients told us that they felt like freaks, because they were the only ones in the world with this disease. I said, "No, it's in my family too, but my family is very small. We need a large family [to test for the gene]. So you're not freaks, but very important!" They were stunned to hear this. They couldn't believe that a country that sent people to the moon could have this disease.

why they wanted these things, especially why they wanted them from seemingly healthy people. Some of the men were also afraid that the sampling procedures would weaken or harm them.

The scientists gave a sort of party for the villagers, during which they tried to explain their work. They found that even pointing out that Wexler, like the Venezuelans, was at risk for the disease brought only disbelief. Then, however, Fidela Gomez, an Argentinean nurse, had an inspiration. She lifted Wexler's arm and led her around the room, showing the people the small scar left after Wexler had given her own skin sample. "See, see, see? She has the mark!" Gomez exclaimed. After that, Wexler reported, the villagers were much more cooperative.

Wexler's team held "draw days" to collect blood samples whenever a member of the team was about to return to the United States. That way, the researcher could carry the samples back. They had to reach the laboratory that would analyze them within 48 hours of being collected. The samples went to Massachusetts General Hospital, where James Gusella, originally a graduate student of Housman's, stored and examined them. Gusella was now in charge of the RFLP project.

By this time, several dozen different RFLPs were known. Gusella started by trying some of them with blood samples from the Iowa family, which were already available. Contrary to the dark predictions of those who had doubted the new technique, Gusella found some evidence that the 12th RFLP he tried, a marker called G8, was inherited along with the Huntington's gene. There were not enough members in the family for him to be sure, however.

Gusella then turned to the samples from the Venezuelans. The results he got were stronger than for the Iowa family. Almost all the Venezuelan family members with Huntington's had inherited one form of the G8 marker, while the healthy members had inherited another form. The odds were better than 1,000 to 1 that this marker was near the Huntington's gene. Gusella and Wexler agreed that he had been amazingly lucky to find the right RFLP so quickly. He and his coworkers published their results in November 1983.

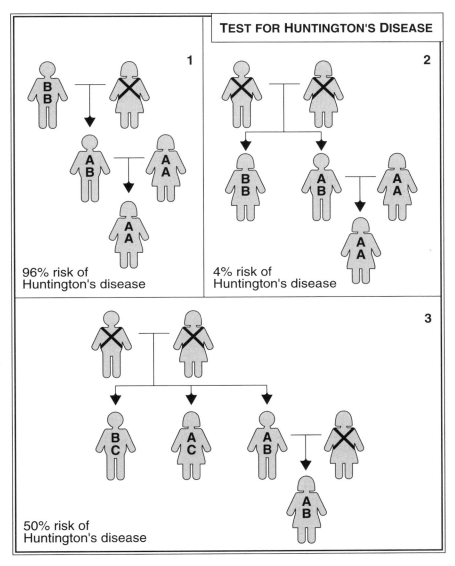

TEST FOR HUNTINGTON'S DISEASE

1
96% risk of Huntington's disease

2
4% risk of Huntington's disease

3
50% risk of Huntington's disease

The first test for Huntington's disease used a marker gene to stand in for the disease gene, which at that time was still unknown. People could inherit several different forms of the marker (shown here as A, B, and C). Research showed that a particular form of the marker would be inherited with the Huntington's gene 96 percent of the time. If a person knows what markers both parents inherited and the markers are different, a test of the person's DNA will show whether he or she is likely to get the disease.

The most immediate result of Gusella's discovery was the creation of a test that showed with about 96 percent certainty whether a person would develop Huntington's disease. The test first began to be used in 1986. Its existence brought Nancy Wexler face to face with a personal dilemma. Did she really want to know whether she would develop the disease that by then had killed her mother? How would she feel, and what would she do, if she tested positive? She had already decided never to have children, so she did not need to know for that reason. Wexler has consistently refused to say whether she has taken the Huntington's test, let alone what the results might have been. If she has decided not to use the test, however, she is far from alone. In the decade after the test came into use, only 13 percent of Americans at risk for the disease took it.

The Twilight Zone of Genetics

Once they found the RFLP marker, Gusella and the other genetic researchers embarked on their next quest: the search for the Huntington's gene itself. Only if the gene was isolated could they identify its protein and begin to learn what produced its deadly effects. To speed the hunt, in 1984 the Hereditary Disease Foundation persuaded research groups at six institutions in the United States and Britain to collaborate on the work. The groups agreed not only to share their research results but to sign scientific papers only with their collective name, the Huntington's Disease Collaborative Research Group.

Such cooperation was almost unheard of, especially in the highly competitive field that genetics had become. Inevitably, the collaboration did not always go smoothly. The scientists involved agree that Nancy Wexler was the glue that held it together. She went from lab to lab, "soothing bruised egos" and "cheering on anyone who was losing momentum."

Wexler also made yearly trips to the Venezuelan family, whom she now regarded as almost her own flesh and blood. During these visits, in addition to collecting more blood samples, she and her group enlarged their knowledge of the villagers' family tree. Today their genealogy diagram covers both walls of the corridor outside Wexler's office at the Columbia University Medical Center in New York City, where she has taught since 1985.

The Venezuelan family tree now includes 10 generations, totalling over 14,000 people. Wexler and her coworkers have established that all of them are descended from one woman, Maria Concepción Soto, who lived in the area in the early 19th century. "From [this] one woman," Wexler has written, "a huge pyramid of suffering has been stretching out over the decades." Family legend claims that Soto inherited the disease from her father, a Spanish sailor. Huntington's disease is found mostly among people of European descent, so the story may be true, but it has never been proved.

Wexler and the others also care for the Venezuelan family as best they can. Américo Negrette, the Venezuelan doctor who first discovered the family, told an interviewer that Wexler

> brings them [the villagers] medicines and . . . projects for their social welfare. . . . She [also] brings them an immeasurable love. . . . I have seen her embracing women and embracing men and kissing children. Without theatre, without simulation, without pose.

Despite the collaborative research group's best efforts, the Huntington's gene remained elusive throughout the 1980s. By 1984 the group had learned that the marker RFLP, and therefore the disease gene, was on the short arm of chromosome 4. It was the first gene mapped to a particular chromosome through RFLP markers alone. Beyond that, though, the group's luck seemed to have run out, even though other scientists found many genes that caused other inherited diseases during this same period.

For many years the Huntington's group thought their quarry was almost at the end of the chromosome arm, a region so difficult to analyze that Wexler had called it "the Twilight Zone of genetics." Then, just as the end region was finally sequenced, evidence

Wexler has learned much from a family in Venezuela in which Huntington's disease is widespread, affecting even children. In return, she has given them what a fellow scientist calls "immeasurable love." (Courtesy Peter Ginter and the Hereditary Disease Foundation)

began suggesting that the gene was in fact farther in on the chromosome. The sequencing had to begin all over again.

The group's quest was finally successful early in 1993. Marcy MacDonald, a senior researcher working with James Gusella, was the one who sequenced the Huntington's gene—and learned what was wrong with it. Near its beginning she found a sort of stutter, a repeating sequence of the bases C-A-G (cytosine-adenine-guanine). The genes of people unaffected by the disease had between 11 and 34 of these repeats. In people who developed Huntington's, however, the repeats numbered 42 or more—sometimes up to 100. The more repeats an affected person's gene had, the sooner in life the disease would appear and the more severe it would be.

Researchers have since found that in its normal form, the Huntington's gene makes a protein that has been given the name huntingtin. This protein's exact function is still unknown, but it seems to affect the way cells make energy. Cells containing the mutant form of the protein seem less able to generate energy than normal ones.

The Ethics of Genetic Testing

The search for an understanding of the Huntington's gene and its protein and, possibly, an eventual way to repair the gene or replace the protein continues. Nancy Wexler follows this research eagerly, but she herself now focuses mostly on the social aspects of inherited diseases. Her particular concern is the effect of testing for diseases like Huntington's, a type of testing sure to become more common as the Human Genome Project and other research identify more genes that cause or increase the risk of disease. In 1989, after James Watson earmarked 3 percent of the genome project's budget for research into the social, legal, and ethical questions that the project would raise, Wexler was chosen to lead the committee that oversees that research.

SOLVING PROBLEMS

NEW TOOLS FOR ANALYZING GENES

New tools developed in the 1980s have made the work of scientists involved in the Human Genome Project much easier. One, a machine invented by Leroy Hood of Caltech in 1986, can work out the base sequence of genes automatically. Another, designed in 1983 by Kary Mullis, who at the time worked for the Cetus Corporation in Emeryville, California, uses a chemical called poly-merase to make many identical copies of a section of DNA molecule very quickly. Mullis calls this process the polymerase chain reaction, or PCR. Scientists continue to develop other tools to automate the tedious work of deciphering genes. At Lawrence Berkeley Laboratory in California, for instance, robots help in several stages of the process.

Wexler strongly supports the genome project itself. It offers the best hope, she says, for both identification and eventual treatment of inherited diseases. Still, she is concerned about what will happen when, as seems likely, the project eventually makes it possible to draw up a complete genetic profile for anyone, showing all the inherited risk factors that will shape the person's life.

Some information from genetic testing can be useful. A woman who knows she has inherited a tendency to develop breast cancer, for instance, might decide to have frequent mammograms (X-ray examinations of the breasts) so that tumors can be detected while they are still small and easily removable. A man with genes that contribute to heart disease might eat a low-fat diet and exercise often to try to counteract the effect of the "bad" genes.

On the other hand, other than helping in decisions about whether to have children, what is the use of knowing that a person has inherited a gene for an incurable disease such as Huntington's? Such knowledge may do far more harm than good,

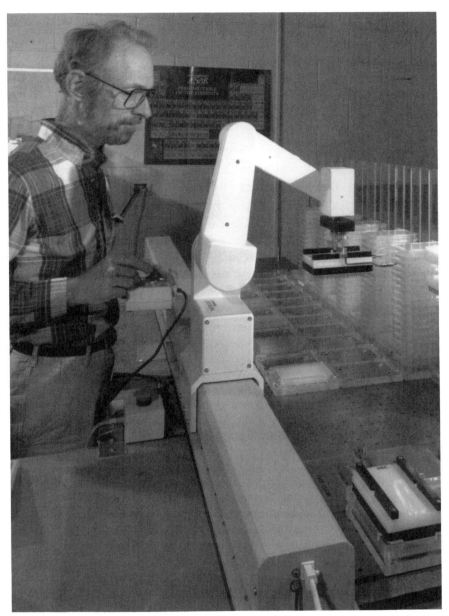

A robot designed by Hewlett-Packard helps to select and reproduce bacterial colonies used to clone genes for the Human Genome Project at the Lawrence Berkeley Laboratory in California. (Courtesy Ernest Orlando Lawrence Berkeley National Laboratory, University of California)

leading to depression or even suicide. Wexler emphasizes that genetic testing should never be given without extensive counseling both before and after the test.

All of Wexler's comments about these issues, like her energetic and productive support of Huntington's disease research, are made more powerful by the public knowledge of her personal drama. Will she escape the tragic fate of her mother? She is now nearing the age at which her mother first learned that she had the disease, but this is later than most people with Huntington's begin to be sick. If Wexler does develop the disease late in life, it may be a less severe form than that which destroyed her mother. And perhaps by the time signs of the illness occur, the research Nancy

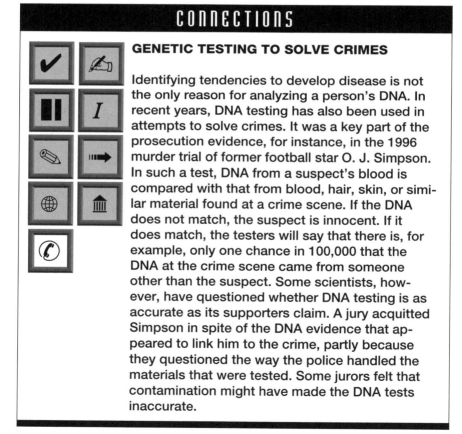

CONNECTIONS

GENETIC TESTING TO SOLVE CRIMES

Identifying tendencies to develop disease is not the only reason for analyzing a person's DNA. In recent years, DNA testing has also been used in attempts to solve crimes. It was a key part of the prosecution evidence, for instance, in the 1996 murder trial of former football star O. J. Simpson. In such a test, DNA from a suspect's blood is compared with that from blood, hair, skin, or similar material found at a crime scene. If the DNA does not match, the suspect is innocent. If it does match, the testers will say that there is, for example, only one chance in 100,000 that the DNA at the crime scene came from someone other than the suspect. Some scientists, however, have questioned whether DNA testing is as accurate as its supporters claim. A jury acquitted Simpson in spite of the DNA evidence that appeared to link him to the crime, partly because they questioned the way the police handled the materials that were tested. Some jurors felt that contamination might have made the DNA tests inaccurate.

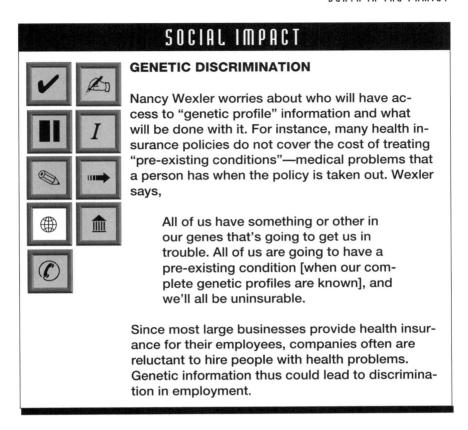

SOCIAL IMPACT

GENETIC DISCRIMINATION

Nancy Wexler worries about who will have access to "genetic profile" information and what will be done with it. For instance, many health insurance policies do not cover the cost of treating "pre-existing conditions"—medical problems that a person has when the policy is taken out. Wexler says,

> All of us have something or other in our genes that's going to get us in trouble. All of us are going to have a pre-existing condition [when our complete genetic profiles are known], and we'll all be uninsurable.

Since most large businesses provide health insurance for their employees, companies often are reluctant to hire people with health problems. Genetic information thus could lead to discrimination in employment.

Wexler has so unstintingly supported will have developed a treatment or a cure.

Chronology of Huntington's Disease

1872	George Huntington describes Huntington's disease
1945	Nancy Wexler born
1967	Folksinger Woody Guthrie dies of Huntington's
1968	Wexler learns that her mother has Huntington's
1974	Hereditary Disease Foundation formed
1976	Wexler chosen to head Congressional committee on Huntington's

1979	Visits family with Huntington's in Venezuela David Housman proposes looking for Huntington's gene by using restriction fragment length polymorphisms (RFLPs)
1981	RFLP work starts
1983	James Gusella discovers RFLP marker for Huntington's gene
1984	Huntington's Disease Collaborative Research Group formed; discovers that Huntington's gene is near end of short arm of chromosome 4
1985	Wexler begins teaching at Columbia University
1986	Test for Huntington's marker first used
1989	Wexler chosen to head ethics committee for Human Genome Project
1993	Huntington's disease gene discovered

Further Reading

Franklin-Barbajosa, Cassandra. "DNA Profiling: The New Science of Identity." *National Geographic*, May 1992. Describes DNA profiling for disease detection, crime investigation, and other purposes.

Human Genome Project home page: World Wide Web: http://www.nchgr.nih.gov/. Offers up-to-date information about the Human Genome Project and a place to comment on the project.

Murray, Mary. "Nancy Wexler." *New York Times Magazine*, February 13, 1994. Extensive article on Wexler and her work, following the discovery of the Huntington's gene.

Picker, Lauren. "All in the Family." *American Health*, March 1994. Good profile of Wexler and description of her research.

Revkin, Andrew. "Hunting Down Huntington's." *Discover*, December 1993. Interesting description of how the Huntington's gene was located.

Wexler, Nancy. "Clairvoyance and Caution: Repercussions from the Human Genome Project." In Daniel J. Kevles and Leroy Hood, eds., *The Code of Codes*. Cambridge, Mass.: Harvard University Press, 1992. Long, interesting article by Wexler describes the search for the Huntington's gene and considers the ethical and social issues raised by genetic testing.

"Wexler, Nancy S." *Current Biography Yearbook 1994*. New York: H. W. Wilson, 1994. Interesting biographical sketch of Wexler, with quotes from interviews.

NOTES

p. 99   "She went from being . . ." Quoted in Lauren Picker. "All in the Family," *American Health*, March 1994, p. 20.

p. 101   "We ask for . . ." Quoted in Andrew Revkin. "Hunting Down Huntington's," *Discover*, December 1993, p. 102.

p. 104   "It was so amazing . . ." Quoted in Mary Murray. "Nancy Wexler," *New York Times Magazine*, February 13, 1994.

p. 105   "We served Coke . . ." Quoted in Maya Pines. "In the Shadow of Huntington's," *Science 84*, May 1984, p. 36.

p. 106   "'See, see, see? . . ." Quoted in Picker, p. 22.

p. 108   "soothing bruised egos . . ." Quoted in "Wexler, Nancy S." *Current Biography Yearbook 1994* (New York: H. W. Wilson, 1994), p. 610.

p. 109   "From [this] one woman . . ." Quoted in Walter Bodmer and Robin McKie. *The Book of Man* (New York: Scribner, 1994), p. 73.

p. 109   "brings them [the villagers] medicines . . ." Quoted in "Wexler, Nancy S.," p. 609.

p. 109   "the Twilight Zone . . ." Quoted in Revkin, p. 108.

p. 115   "All of us have . . ." Quoted in Picker, p. 24.

7

New Genes for Old

FRENCH ANDERSON AND GENE THERAPY

A visiting professor once called W. French Anderson a daydreamer, but Anderson has made his dream of treating human disease by altering genes come true. (Courtesy Bill Youngblood and the University of Southern California)

In 1958, just five years after James Watson and Francis Crick had described the structure of DNA, a Harvard graduate student attended a seminar. He listened to a visiting professor describe new discoveries about the structure of hemoglobin, the red protein in the blood that carries oxygen.

Unlike most of his classmates, this student had a comment. "If it is possible to work out the structure of normal hemoglobin," he said,

> then maybe you can work out the structure of sickle cell hemoglobin [the defective hemoglobin produced by people with sickle cell anemia, a common inherited disease], and then you could determine what the defect is. And . . . maybe you could put in the gene for normal hemoglobin, and correct sickle cell hemoglobin.

The professor was not interested in such a novel idea. "This is a serious scientific discussion," he snapped. "If you want to daydream, keep it to yourself!"

The remark hurt, of course. It did not stop W. French Anderson from daydreaming about curing human disease by replacing damaged genes, however. Nor did it persuade him to keep his idea to himself. Instead, he pursued his dream of gene therapy relentlessly until, in 1990, he began to make it come true. In that year, for the first time, a child with an inherited disease was started on the road to health by a change made in her genes.

A Boyhood Dream

Born in Tulsa, Oklahoma, in 1936, Anderson, like James Watson, was a precocious child. While his classmates struggled with grade-school readers, he devoured college textbooks. His bookish ways and conviction that "everyone else was stupid" left him with few

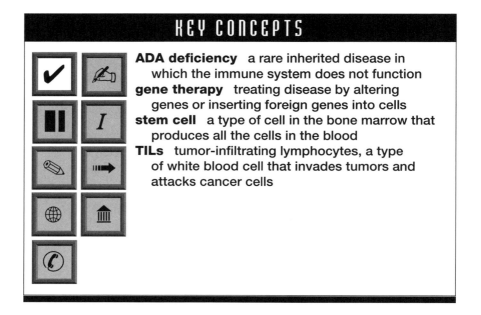

KEY CONCEPTS

ADA deficiency   a rare inherited disease in which the immune system does not function

gene therapy   treating disease by altering genes or inserting foreign genes into cells

stem cell   a type of cell in the bone marrow that produces all the cells in the blood

TILs   tumor-infiltrating lymphocytes, a type of white blood cell that invades tumors and attacks cancer cells

friends. In fact, a fifth-grade classmate told him that he was the most unpopular boy in school.

Anderson decided to change that. First, to mark his new personality, he changed the name he used from Bill (for his first name, William) to his middle name, French. He then set about making friends with the same energy and determination that he would later use to blaze the trail for a new medical treatment. By seventh grade he was popular enough to be elected class president. He also later became a track star and—in spite of a stutter—a member of the debating team.

French Anderson had planned to be a doctor since he was 10 years old. By the time he finished high school, he knew that his main interest was in research. In his application to Harvard in 1953, a time when few people knew that molecular biology existed, he wrote, "I want to understand disease at the molecular level."

From the beginning, Anderson worked with top scientists. He met James Watson at Harvard and did graduate work under Francis Crick at Cambridge, where he also met his future wife,

Kathy. In 1965 he moved to the NIH and joined the laboratory of Marshall Nirenberg, the leader among the researchers deciphering the genetic code. Anderson's enthusiasm and reliability soon made Nirenberg call him his "right-hand man."

Anderson got his first chance to help people with an inherited disease in 1968. The disease was a rare blood disorder called thalassemia. Because of a defect in the genes that make hemoglobin, red blood cells in people with thalassemia die much sooner than they should. The people's tissues therefore never get enough oxygen. In a sense, thalassemics slowly suffocate. Without treatment, they die at an early age.

Frequent blood transfusions could keep people with thalassemia alive, but the transfusions shut down the production of hemoglobin in their bodies. As a result, iron, which is normally used in making hemoglobin, accumulated in their liver and other

CONNECTIONS

GOOD NEWS-BAD NEWS GENES

Scientists have discovered an interesting possible reason why some inherited diseases, including thalassemia, have survived so long in certain populations, even though they cause death at a young age. In these disorders, only people who inherit two copies of a defective gene become sick. Those who inherit one copy may actually have better health than those with completely normal genes. For instance, people who inherit one gene for thalassemia or for sickle-cell anemia appear to be protected against malaria, a serious blood disease caused by a microorganism. These inherited blood disorders usually occur in people whose ancestors came from the Mediterranean Sea or Africa, where malaria is common. The mutated genes thus may have given their carriers an evolutionary advantage, even though some of their children died.

tissues. Excess iron is a poison, and in time it killed thalassemics just as surely as a lack of red cells would have. French Anderson, however, found a drug that removed iron molecules from the body. It greatly extended the lives of thalassemic patients.

Anderson's work with thalassemia was so successful that he got his own laboratory at NIH. In 1974, however, he stopped this line of research because it was not bringing him closer to his ultimate goal. "If I wanted to do gene therapy, I had to give up all this stuff," he said later.

When genetic engineering became possible, the dream of gene therapy moved much closer to reality. Indeed, in 1980 one eager doctor tried to use gene repair to treat thalassemia, the same disease Anderson had worked with. Martin Cline of the University of California at Los Angeles asked the NIH's Recombinant DNA Advisory Committee (RAC) for permission to try to put normal hemoglobin genes into thalassemic patients, but the committee refused. Cline then went to Europe and tried the treatment there. He failed to get the genes into the patients' blood cells, however. Worse still, his premature attempt put the whole idea of gene therapy in a bad light for many scientists.

The "Bubble Boy" Disease

After years of frustration, French Anderson's research picked up speed in 1984 after he heard about a new way of introducing genes into cells. It used nature's genetic engineers, the retroviruses. Richard Mulligan of the Massachusetts Institute of Technology (MIT) found a way to alter a retrovirus that caused cancer in mice so that the virus could not multiply or cause disease but could still infect cells. If a foreign gene was attached to the altered virus's genome, the virus would insert that gene into the cell genome along with its own. Anderson thought the virus would be a fine vector, or carrier, for human genes.

But which inherited disease should he treat? It had to be a disease caused by a defect in just one gene, because inserting even a single gene into cells and getting it to work would be tricky. That ruled out diseases caused by defects in hemoglobin, such as thalassemia and sickle-cell anemia, because several genes are involved in making hemoglobin. The disease's gene had to be known, so that many copies of it could be made. Finally, it had to be a disease whose genetic cure would be effective if inserted into a relatively small number of cells that could easily be extracted from and returned to the body. The main cells that fitted this description were blood cells.

Only a few inherited diseases met all these requirements. After some consideration, Anderson focused on one called ADA deficiency. This disease was very rare, affecting only about 40 children worldwide at any given time, but it was deadly. The cells of people with ADA deficiency could not make a cell chemical called adenosine deaminase (ADA). Without this chemical to break them down, certain other substances piled up in the cells.

These accumulated substances cause no harm to most cells, but they are poisonous to certain types of white blood cells that play a key role in the immune system. As a result, children with ADA deficiency essentially had no immune system. Like people with AIDS, they were sick almost constantly because their bodies lacked a way to fight off microbes. Most of these children died before they were two years old. The disease's best-known victim, a Texas boy named David, spent his life in a plastic "bubble" to protect him from microbes. Even so, he died in 1984, when he was only 12.

Knowing Anderson's interest in ADA deficiency, his wife, a surgeon who specialized in treating children, introduced him to another NIH scientist named Michael Blaese. Blaese was an expert in ADA deficiency and other childhood immune diseases. He and Anderson began working together in 1984.

Anderson and Blaese agreed that the best way to treat ADA deficiency would be to insert the gene for making ADA into stem cells. These cells, found in the bone marrow, produce all the types of blood cells. Stem cells live as long as a person does, so a gene change in them should remain effective throughout a patient's life.

Blaese, Anderson, and their coworkers tried to get retroviruses to carry the ADA gene into human and animal stem cells. They had little luck. Then, in mid-1987, a new project member named Kenneth Culver put the gene into white blood cells instead. This proved to be an easier task, and the treated cells made much more ADA than the stem cells had. White cells do not live as long as stem cells, but some kinds survive for a decade or more. The researchers decided that if they could get the ADA gene into some of these cells, their treatment might be almost as good as one involving stem cells.

While Culver and other team members struggled with the technical difficulties of the ADA project, Anderson took on the political ones. Steven Lindow had to undergo a years-long struggle to gain approval from the RAC and other government agencies before he could test his ice-minus bacteria, and Anderson knew that he would have to jump over far more hurdles before he would be allowed to put altered genes into humans. Early in 1987 he offered the RAC his first proposal for treating ADA-deficient

OTHER SCIENTISTS

KENNETH CULVER

Kenneth Culver (1955–   ) was the youngest major member of the ADA project. He had the most direct experience in working with children. He was also an expert on bone marrow cells. He did much of the laboratory work involved in the project, and, when a human patient finally was treated, he was the one who took care of her. More recently, Culver has worked on a gene-therapy treatment for brain cancer. By inserting a gene from a herpes virus into brain tumor cells, he makes the cells sensitive to Gancyclovir, a drug used to treat herpes infections. Most anticancer drugs cannot be used in the brain, but Gancyclovir can.

humans with gene therapy, a document more than 500 pages long. He expected it to be rejected, and it was. The process, however, told him what questions he would have to answer before he could proceed.

In late 1987 another obstacle appeared: a new treatment for ADA deficiency that seemed far less risky than gene therapy. ADA could not be given to patients directly, as insulin is given to diabetics, because it quickly broke down in the bloodstream. Michael Hershfield of Duke University, however, found a way to coat ADA from cattle with a substance called polyethylene glycol. The resulting drug, PEG-ADA, was not destroyed by the body. Weekly injections of PEG-ADA allowed some ADA-deficient children to lead relatively normal lives. Anderson noted, though, that the drug did not help all children with the disease. He still hoped he could persuade the RAC to let him try gene therapy with children who did not respond to PEG-ADA.

A Small Step, a Giant Leap

Blaese and Anderson now realized that the best first step toward human gene therapy might not involve treatment of disease at all. In order to gain RAC approval, the first introduction of altered genes into people would have to be an experiment whose safety was almost beyond question. In 1988, Blaese found what seemed to be the perfect candidate. The experiment would help a fellow NIH scientist and, at the same time, provide a wedge that might open the RAC's door to more ambitious proposals.

Blaese introduced Anderson to the other scientist, Steven A. Rosenberg, in March. Rosenberg was chief of surgery at the National Cancer Institute. He had discovered that one kind of white cells, which he called tumor-infiltrating lymphocytes (TILs), moved into tumors and attacked cancer cells. Unless a tumor was very small, however, the body could not muster enough TILs to destroy it. Rosenberg was looking for ways to make the TILs more effective.

The first method Rosenberg tried was to take blood from cancer patients, remove some of the white cells, and return the blood to them. He then separated the TILs from the other white cells and grew them in his laboratory. To the culture medium he added a growth hormone called interleukin-2, which made the TILs multiply rapidly. When their number was greatly increased, he reinjected them into the patients.

Rosenberg's treatment shrank tumors at least for a while in about 40 percent of the terminally ill patients on whom he tried it. It completely cured a few. The rest, however, were not helped, and Rosenberg wanted to learn why. In order to do so, he needed to know what happened to the cells after they reentered the patients' bodies. This meant he needed some way to mark the cells so that they could be traced.

Radioactive tracers could not be safely left in the body long enough to give Rosenberg the information he wanted. Blaese, however, suggested that adding a gene to the TILs while they were in the laboratory might do the trick. The gene he recommended was a bacterial one that conferred resistance to an antibiotic called neomycin. It could be carried into the cells in a retrovirus. The gene was not expected to have any effect on either the patients or their cancers. Because of this, and because the group proposed to treat only patients who were expected to die within a few months, the scientists thought they had a better chance of getting RAC approval for this experiment than for one that attempted to produce changes in the body.

The group first applied to the RAC and the Food and Drug Administration (FDA), which also had to approve the project, in June 1988. Their plan was rejected. The scientists on the committees wanted more information and more animal tests to assure that the procedure would be safe. Antigenetic gadfly Jeremy Rifkin, who had caused so much trouble for Steven Lindow, also staged protests against the project.

Anderson, Blaese, and Rosenberg finally got the permissions they needed. On May 22, 1989, they began dripping a flow of TILs, now enriched with the neomycin-resistance gene, into a man with advanced melanoma, a deadly skin cancer. He was the

ISSUES

WHERE SHOULD GENE THERAPY STOP?

Jeremy Rifkin protested against gene therapy, not because he thought the therapy itself was dangerous, but because he feared that in the future it might be misused. He wrote in his 1983 book, *Algeny*,

> Once we decide to begin the process of human genetic engineering, there really is no logical place to stop. If diabetes, sickle-cell disease, and cancer are to be cured by altering the genetic makeup of an individual, why not proceed to other "disorders": myopia [nearsightedness], color blindness, left handedness. Indeed, what is to preclude a society from deciding that a certain skin color is a disorder?

Many people share Rifkin's concern. On the other hand, one mother of a child with sickle-cell anemia, who might someday benefit from gene therapy, has said that people like Rifkin are "simplistic moralists who probably have seen too many mad scientist horror films."

first person ever to receive foreign genes. Just after the experiment began, someone put up a sign in Anderson's lab. Echoing astronaut Neil Armstrong's first words after stepping onto the moon, it read, "That was one small step for a gene, but a giant leap for genetics."

As expected, the treatment did not help this patient or the other nine people who received it. Unfortunately, it also failed to give Rosenberg any new insights about the TIL treatment. It did, however, succeed in marking the cells. It also helped Anderson prove the safety of gene therapy: the patients showed no additional problems that could be traced to the altered cells.

A Girl Called Ashanthi

Rosenberg was now converted to the idea of gene therapy. As a start, he hoped to insert a gene for making a substance called tumor necrosis factor (TNF) into his TILs. While he worked on this project, Anderson, Blaese, and Culver went back to their plans to use gene therapy to treat ADA deficiency. Blaese knew about most of the ADA-deficient children in the United States, and he asked their doctors to send him samples of their blood. He wanted to see which ones had white cells that grew well in laboratory cultures. A successful treatment would require such growth.

Blaese's tests suggested that the most promising child to receive the pioneering therapy was a solemn, round-faced three-year-old named Ashanthi deSilva. She and her parents, Raj and Van deSilva, lived in Ohio, where Raj was a chemist. Ashanthi's parents kept her at home, separated from other children, in the hope of preventing the constant infections she had suffered almost since

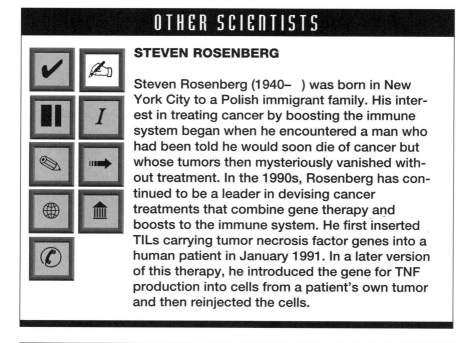

OTHER SCIENTISTS

STEVEN ROSENBERG

Steven Rosenberg (1940–) was born in New York City to a Polish immigrant family. His interest in treating cancer by boosting the immune system began when he encountered a man who had been told he would soon die of cancer but whose tumors then mysteriously vanished without treatment. In the 1990s, Rosenberg has continued to be a leader in devising cancer treatments that combine gene therapy and boosts to the immune system. He first inserted TILs carrying tumor necrosis factor genes into a human patient in January 1991. In a later version of this therapy, he introduced the gene for TNF production into cells from a patient's own tumor and then reinjected the cells.

birth. She received regular PEG-ADA shots, but they seemed to do her little good.

Blaese and the other scientists began talking to the deSilvas in May 1990. They explained what they wanted to do and how the treatment might help Ashanthi. They also described the risks involved. It was possible, for instance, that the carrier virus might combine with existing viruses in the child's body and recover its ability to multiply or cause cancer. Alternatively, the virus might happen to insert its genetic cargo in the middle of a tumor suppressor gene, destroying it, or next to an oncogene, waking it to life. Either way, the result again might be cancer. Neither of these events seemed likely, but the parents had to know they could happen. After much discussion, the deSilvas agreed to accept the risks and let Ashanthi take the treatment.

Meanwhile, Anderson was struggling once again with the RAC and the FDA, not to mention Jeremy Rifkin. Some committee members still had strong doubts about the proposed treatment. In the end, Anderson's group had to wade through eight months of reviews by seven committees before gaining final approval.

A Historic Treatment

At the beginning of September 1990, Ashanthi deSilva and her parents came to NIH. Kenneth Culver removed blood from her arm. The white cells were filtered out of the blood, and the red cells and fluid were returned to her body. The white cells were then taken to the laboratory, mixed with the altered virus containing the ADA gene, and allowed to multiply for 10 days.

On September 14, just a few days past her fourth birthday, Ashanthi made medical history as she watched *Sesame Street* on the television near her hospital bed. In the course of about half an hour, a billion or so of her own white blood cells dripped through a tube and needle into a vein in her hand. The procedure was much like an ordinary blood transfusion. This time, though, Anderson

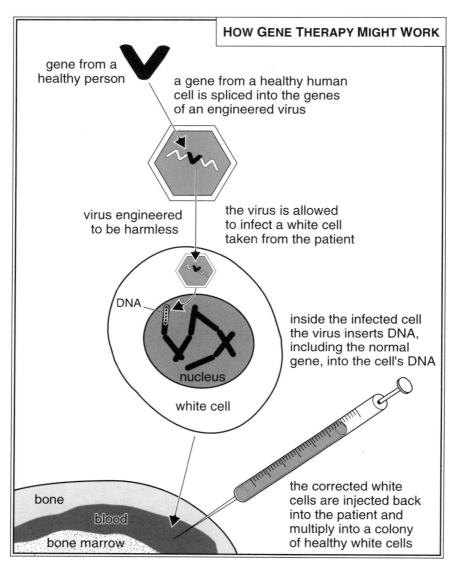

HOW GENE THERAPY MIGHT WORK

gene from a healthy person

a gene from a healthy human cell is spliced into the genes of an engineered virus

virus engineered to be harmless

the virus is allowed to infect a white cell taken from the patient

DNA

inside the infected cell the virus inserts DNA, including the normal gene, into the cell's DNA

nucleus

white cell

bone

blood

bone marrow

the corrected white cells are injected back into the patient and multiply into a colony of healthy white cells

To treat Ashanthi deSilva, French Anderson and his coworkers used genetic engineering techniques to splice a human gene that makes ADA (dark segment) into the genome of a retrovirus. The virus had been modified so that it could not reproduce or cause disease. White cells were then removed from Ashanthi's blood and grown in laboratory dishes. The virus was added to the dishes and infected some of the cells, inserting the ADA gene into them along with its own RNA. When the cells were injected back into Ashanthi, the new gene began making ADA in her body, allowing her immune system to function.

and the other scientists at her bedside hoped that many of the cells were carrying the lifesaving ADA gene.

Addressing reporters who had gathered for the occasion, French Anderson pointed out that the science behind the treatment had been known since the mid-1980s. This moment, he said, was not so much a scientific triumph as "a cultural breakthrough, . . . an event that changes the way that we as a society think about ourselves." From then on, people would see their genes, not as a legacy that must be accepted, but as something that potentially could be changed at will.

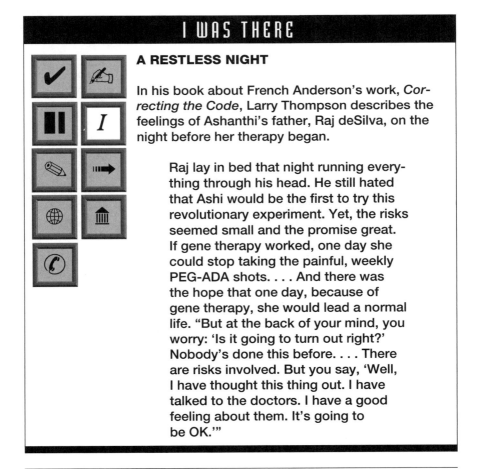

I WAS THERE

A RESTLESS NIGHT

In his book about French Anderson's work, *Correcting the Code*, Larry Thompson describes the feelings of Ashanthi's father, Raj deSilva, on the night before her therapy began.

> Raj lay in bed that night running everything through his head. He still hated that Ashi would be the first to try this revolutionary experiment. Yet, the risks seemed small and the promise great. If gene therapy worked, one day she could stop taking the painful, weekly PEG-ADA shots. . . . And there was the hope that one day, because of gene therapy, she would lead a normal life. "But at the back of your mind, you worry: 'Is it going to turn out right?' Nobody's done this before. . . . There are risks involved. But you say, 'Well, I have thought this thing out. I have talked to the doctors. I have a good feeling about them. It's going to be OK.'"

The gene therapy designed by W. French Anderson and other scientists at the National Institutes of Health changed Ashanthi deSilva from a sickly child into a lively girl who "loves life and does everything.*" Here, Anderson and Ashanthi walk down a hospital corridor together.* (Courtesy Van deSilva and the University of Southern California)

Ashanthi's gene treatment had to be repeated every month at first. She also continued to receive PEG-ADA shots. After a few years, though, the scientists found that one cell treatment a year was enough. The dose of PEG-ADA could be cut in half. The ADA gene, it seemed, had gotten into some of Ashanthi's long-lived white cells, and they were multiplying and replacing the defective cells.

Laboratory tests showed that Ashanthi's immune system improved steadily. She gained energy and suffered fewer infections. She began attending school, playing with friends, and generally leading the life of a normal child. In 1995, Anderson wrote,

> With the help of occasional follow-up treatments, [Ashanthi] has now been transformed from a quarantine little girl, who was always sick and left the house only to visit her doctor, into a healthy, vibrant nine-year-old who loves life and does *everything*.

Results with a second ADA-deficient child, Cynthia Cutshall, were equally encouraging. In more recent years, furthermore, Michael Blaese and other scientists have worked out ways to put the ADA gene into stem cells, the targets they originally wanted to reach.

Where Gene Therapy Is Going

Today, more than 40 types of experimental gene therapy are in progress around the world. They include treatments for inherited diseases, cancer, and AIDS. Not all of the treatments have worked as well as the ones given to Ashanthi, but none has seriously harmed its recipients. All have helped researchers learn more about the best way to perform this new kind of medical care. Improvements continue to be invented, including ways to introduce genes without using viruses and ways to make the added genes function in more cells.

SOCIAL IMPACT

THE DANGERS OF GERM-LINE THERAPY

Many geneticists, including French Anderson, agree that human gene therapy should be applied only to cells of an individual's body. Even if the technology to do so is perfected, such treatment should not be applied to the germ line—the genes of the sex cells, which will be passed on to a person's offspring. For one thing, scientists know too little about what genes do. By removing a gene that causes a disease, they may also remove a trait that is, or may be, useful in some way. An even greater fear is that germ-line treatment might be used in a new form of eugenics, an attempt to redesign the human species itself.

As the Human Genome Project uncovers more disease-causing genes and better genetic engineering techniques are developed, gene therapy is likely to become more common. Genetically engineered cells might be used as drug delivery systems, providing insulin to diabetics, for example. French Anderson looks forward to a day when corrective genes can be injected as easily as antibiotics are today.

Anderson recently told an interviewer,

> Every disease has a genetic component. . . . So [gene therapy] . . . will be applicable to every disease. . . . What makes gene therapy particularly exciting isn't curing them [diseases], it's preventing them. . . . If a person has a propensity [tendency], for example, for breast cancer, you simply supply her with the correct version of the gene so she never gets cancer. . . . That's where gene therapy is going.

If gene therapy reaches this goal, it will be in large part because of the persistence and determination of the onetime Harvard "daydreamer," French Anderson.

Chronology of Gene Therapy

1936	French Anderson born in Tulsa, Oklahoma
1965	Joins Marshall Nirenberg's laboratory at NIH
1968	Begins work on thalassemia
1980	Martin Cline makes premature attempt to use gene therapy
1984	Richard Mulligan invents way to alter retrovirus to make it a safe vector for carrying genes
	Anderson begins plans to treat ADA deficiency
1987	First proposal to treat people with ADA deficiency rejected by RAC
	Kenneth Culver invents way to get ADA gene into white cells
	PEG-ADA, drug to treat ADA deficiency, created
1988	Anderson, Blaese, and Steven Rosenberg plan to use added gene as marker in cancer treatment
1989	Foreign genes inserted into humans for first time
1990	Foreign genes used successfully to treat disease

Further Reading

Anderson, W. French. "Gene Therapy." *Scientific American*, September 1995. Describes technique of altering genes to treat disease. Moderately difficult reading.

"Anderson, W. French." *Current Biography Yearbook 1994*. New York: H. W. Wilson, 1994. Good biographical article on Anderson, with quotes from interviews.

Elmer-Dewitt, Philip. "The Genetic Revolution." *Time*, January 17, 1994. Several related articles on genetics and gene therapy, including material on French Anderson.

Henig, Robin Marantz. "Dr. Anderson's Gene Machine." *New York Times Magazine*, March 31, 1991. Extensive interview

with Anderson and description of his work, including treatment of Ashanthi deSilva.

McAuliffe, Kathleen. "Interview: W. French Anderson." *Omni*
July 1991. Interview discusses Anderson's work in treating
ADA deficiency and his ideas about gene therapy.

Rosenberg, Steven A. *The Transformed Cell.* New York: G. P.
Putnam's Sons, 1992. Describes Rosenberg's cancer experiments, including those he did with Anderson and subsequent
ones involving gene therapy.

Thompson, Larry. *Correcting the Code.* New York: Simon and
Schuster, 1994. Focuses on French Anderson's work but also
describes the advances in molecular biology and genetic engineering that have made gene therapy possible.

NOTES

p. 119   "If it is possible . . ." Quoted in Larry Thompson. *Correcting the Code*
(New York: Simon and Schuster, 1994), p. 87.

p. 119   "everyone else was stupid." Quoted in Robin Marantz Henig. "Dr.
Anderson's Gene Machine," *New York Times Magazine*, March 31,
1991.

p. 120   "I want to understand . . ." Quoted in Henig, p. 33.

p. 121   "right-hand man." Quoted in Thompson, p. 96.

p. 122   "If I wanted . . ." Quoted in Thompson, pp. 112–13.

p. 127   "Once we decide . . ." Quoted in Richard Golob and Eric Brus, eds.
The Almanac of Science and Technology (Boston: Harcourt Brace
Jovanovich, 1990), p. 120.

p. 127   "simplistic moralists . . ." Quoted in Golob, p. 121.

p. 127   "That was one small step . . ." Quoted in Thompson, p. 300.

p. 131   "a cultural breakthrough, . . ." Quoted in Joseph Levine and David
Suzuki. *The Secret of Life* (Boston: WGBH Educational Foundation,
1993), p. 207.

p. 131   "Raj lay in bed . . ." Quoted in Thompson, p. 40.

p. 144   "With the help . . ." W. French Anderson. "Gene Therapy," *Scientific American*, September 1995, p. 124.

p. 134   "Every disease . . ." Quoted in Levine and Suzuki, p. 216.

Index

Numbers in *italics* indicate illustrations. Numbers in **boldface** indicate major treatment of a topic.

E

EcoR1 60–61

egg *see* sex cells

Eichling, C. W. 11

environment

as cancer cause 85, *90*, 94–95

effect of genetically engineered organisms on 72–73

importance of in determining characteristics ix–x, 2, 12

Escherichia coli 60–62, 64, *65*

eugenics 16, 33, 134

evolution x, 2–4, 10–16, 23, 33, 34, 86, 121

"Experiments in Plant Hybridization" (Mendel paper) 11

F

factors (early name for genes) 8, 10, 15, 20, 22

farming, genetic engineering in 70, 74–75

Fisher, Ronald 9

Flavr Savr tomato 74

Flemming, Walther 21–22

"Fly Room" 19–20, 24, 27–28, 31, 103

Food and Drug Administration (FDA) 70, 126, 129

Franklin, Rosalind 41, 44–45

Friend, Stephen H. 93

frost

damage to plants 70

protection against 71–73

fruit flies 19–20, 24–29, 31–34, 61, 68

G

Gallo, Robert 82

Galton, Francis 16

Gancyclovir 124

Garrod, Archibald 101

Genentech 67–69

genes

amplification 89

analyzing 69, 112, *113*

changing *see* genetic engineering, gene therapy

chemical nature of 38–39, 51

chromosomes, location on 22, 28, 31, 102–103, 109, 111

code of 51, 121

germ-line 134

in cancer x, 34, 53, 64, 79, 82–97, 112

linkage 28–29, 31, 103

patenting 68

searches for 51, 102–106, 108–109, 111

structure of 40, 44–45, *46*

term introduced 15

testing for 105, *107*, 108, 111–112, 114–115

gene splicing *see* genetic engineering

gene therapy *xi, 53, 118–120, 122–136*

chronology 135

ethical concerns 127, 134

for ADA deficiency 123–125, 128–133

for cancer 124, 127–128, 133, 134

further reading 135–136

future of 134

technique 122, *130*